~ THE ~
SAD BASTARD
COOKBOOK

FOOD YOU CAN MAKE SO YOU DON'T DIE

By Zilla Novikov & Rachel A. Rosen
Illustrated by Marten Norr

The Sad Bastard Cookbook
Food you can make so you don't die
By Zilla Novikov & Rachel A. Rosen
Illustrated by Marten Norr

Copyright © 2022 Zilla Novikov & Rachel A. Rosen.

Creative Commons License
This work is licensed under a Creative Commons Attribution-NonCommercial-ShareAlike 4.0 International License.

ISBN: 978-1-80352-120-6 (Paperback)

Any references to historical events, real people, or real places are used fictitiously. All trademarks and copyrighted items mentioned and shown in photos are the property of their respective owners. Names, characters, and places are products of the authors' imagination. The authors have pretty vivid imaginations.

Cover photos and book design by Rachel A. Rosen.
Illustrations by Marten Norr.

Independent Publishing Network

A proud part of the *Night Beats* Extended Universe.
Come join us!
www.nightbeatseu.ca

TABLE OF CONTENTS

Content notes: Mental and physical illness, disordered eating, and dark humour throughout, as well as occasional mentions of alcohol, swearing, and political references. If you have specific food triggers, some recipes may be unpalatable to you.

Recipes which have vegan core ingredients are marked with a (V).

We're so meta that we include the Table of Contents in the Table of Contents. Lev would approve.

Table of Contents
Introduction... 7
Ramen Variations Part 1: Classic Ramen (V) 11
Ramen Variations Part II: Instant Noodles on a Plate (V) 15
Ramen Variations Part III: Apocalypse Ramen (V) 17
Kinda Like Pad Thai (V) 19
Pasta Variations (V) 20
Literal Depression Cooking 24
Pasta in a Rice Cooker (V) 25
Eggy Pasta... 26
Pasta with Homemade Tomato Sauce (V) 27
Pasta with One (1) Actual Vegetable (V) 28
Spaghetti Aglio e Olio (V) 30
Mac & Cheese.. 31
Rice Variations Part I: Cook the Rice (V) 33
Rice Variations Part II: Add Stuff to the Cooking Water (V) 36
Rice Variations Part III: Add Stuff to the Cooked Rice (V) 38
Another Rice Variation: Black Beans & Rice (V) 40
Rice Variations Part IV: Fried Rice (V) 42
Fried Noodles (V) 44
Couscous Variations (V) 46
Potato Variations Part I: Baked (V) 48
Potato Variations Part II: Boiled (V) 50
Potato Variations Part III: Mashed (V) 51

Potato Variations Part IV: French Fries (V) 52
French Fry Variations: Now What? (V) 54
Spring Rolls (V) 57
Hangover Bubble and Squeak (V) 59
Roasted Vegetables (V) 61
Pancakes (V) 63
Korean-Inspired Pancakes (V) 67
Oatmeal Variations (V) 69
The Humble Egg 71
Chinese-Style Eggs & Tomato 74
Eggs & Bread Variations 75
Bean Salad (V) 77
Lentils in a Pot (V) 78
Cheater Chana Masala (V) 80
Can of Soup (V) 81
Dumplings (V) 83
Pierogi (V) 85
Peanut Butter on a Spoon (V) 87
Peanut Butter Balls (V) 88
Apple Slices Yes (V) 89
Grapefruit No (V) 90
Eat a Dill Pickle Out of the Jar While Standing in Front of the Fridge (V) 91
Popcorn (V) 92
Eddy No (V) 93
Chips (V) 94
College Guacamole (V) 95
The Fastest Nachos (V) 96
Quesadillas & Pumpki-dillas Part I: The Basics (V) 98
Quesadillas & Pumpki-dillas Part II: Variations (V) 100
Wraps (V) 101
Toast Variations (V) 103
Crackers and Stuff (V) 105
Fancy Cheese and Crackers 106
Hummus (V) 107
Garlic Bread (V) 108
Tostadas Con Tomate (V) 109
Grilled Cheese Sandwiches 110

"Pizza" (V) 112
Tanzanian Braised Coconut Cabbage (V) 113
Bag Salad (V) 114
Cabbage Salads (V) 116
Ants on a Log (V) 118
Fried Plantains (V) 119
Smoothie Variations (V) 120
Ice Cream (V) 122
Moroccan Oranges (V) 123
"Baked" Apples (V) 124
Banana Frozen Yogurt 125
"Parfait" 126
Chocolate Pudding (V) 127
Core Ingredients to Keep in Your Kitchen 129
Zilla's Shopping List & Weekly Menu 132
Rachel's "Three Meals a Day Are Cognitive Overload"
  Shopping List & Weekly Menu 135
Thank You to Our Contributors 139
Message from the Authors 141
Not an Index 143

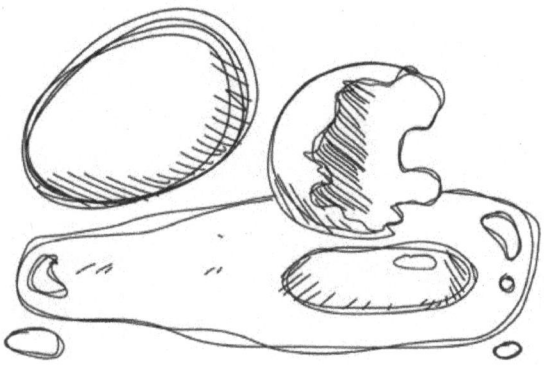

5

INTRODUCTION

Every cookbook says that it's different. One promises to have you eating healthy, another as your ancient ancestors did, a third to demystify foam. This cookbook isn't like that.

Hey, Blythe from Cascade, stop letting Jonah pull this one.

This cookbook is an old friend who keeps crashing on your couch, promising they've got something lined up and are gonna get their shit together. This cookbook is all the recipes you already make, when you've worked a 16-hour day, when you can't stop crying and you don't know why, when the eldritch abomination you woke at the bottom of the ocean won't go back to sleep. And hopefully, this cookbook gives you some new meal ideas. Even Sad Bastards have to eat.

We promise these recipes are:

* Simple. Like, add boiling water and eat simple. We don't care if you can't maintain focus. You are the target audience for this cookbook. There are options for Next Level cooking, going up to God-Tier difficulty for the best-worst days, but there's also Peanut Butter on a Spoon for the worst-worst days.

* Ingredients which (mostly) don't go bad. We see you. Maybe you're too busy to keep up with the groceries, maybe you're just too depressed. Treat yourself to a meal with fresh vegetables on grocery day! But people who shop mostly in the canned, dried, and frozen food aisles can go a lot longer between grocery runs.

* Cheap. The Boomers destroyed the economy. Sorry to any Boomers reading this. We don't like that you did it either. #NotAllBoomers. But if you voted for Reagan, Mulroney, or Thatcher and you don't regret it, this cookbook isn't for you.

* Vegetarian or vegan. Because the two of us writing this cookbook are veg, and we can't test recipes we won't eat. Besides, the world is falling apart and the last thing you need is food poisoning.

Dany from Sushi and Sea Lions, take note. Raw chicken is not good date food.

- Tasty. Yes, you deserve good food. Don't try to argue with us. We don't care what you think. You are worthy of love and worthy of eating food that makes you happy.

How this cookbook will work:

- Meals typically have a core recipe and optional variations which you can use to keep things interesting.

- Core ingredients will be listed at the top of each recipe. Those are things you absolutely need to cook each recipe. For example, it's literally impossible to make _Bean Salad_ without beans.

  Well, you can add cheese to literally anything at all, but it's probably not good on Chocolate Pudding.

- Meals where the core recipe is vegan are marked with a Ⓥ. Lots of these will have vegetarian options—you can add cheese to almost anything and then it's not vegan. A few of the core recipes are vegetarian, not vegan. We're sorry, but we couldn't figure out how to make _The Humble Egg_ both vegan and low effort. But vegans should still find plenty of tasty things in this book.

  We checked and Piers Morgan's tears count as vegan.

- The order of the recipes is intensely chaotic. We tried so hard to impose a structure, but it turns out that's even harder to do in a cookbook than it is in genre-bending fiction. Is _Peanut Butter on a Spoon_ an appetizer, a main meal, or a dessert? Are _Peanut Butter Balls_ a variation of _Peanut Butter on a Spoon_, or are they distinct enough to count as a different recipe? If you've got the e-version of the book, we recommend you use the search function to find recipes which use specific ingredients. If you only have the paper version, you can get the e-version for free from our website www.nightbeatseu.ca. Hey, did you know we have a website?

- At the end of this book, we have listed our personal top picks for Core Ingredients to Keep in Your Kitchen. These are things that you can stock up on when you're in decent enough shape to go grocery shopping. It's not an exhaustive list—it's just our ideas for what we keep around.

- We also list Shopping Lists to go with Weekly Menus. Making decisions is hard. We thought you might like it if we made some for you.

- Despite our deep and abiding love for food, our background is in fiction. Rachel's published Cascade (The Sleep of Reason Book 1), Zilla's got Query published, and Marten's written a queer steampunk novel you're going to adore. There are a lot more great novels, novellas, short stories, and games by other members of the Night Beats community, and we all shamelessly love pop culture. We couldn't resist writing jokes in the margins of this cookbook. If you don't find them funny or haven't read the books, the recipes will work anyway.

- This book will tell you that you should eat, because eating is good, and you are good. There are very few other "shoulds" in this book. If you avoid carbs when you're in the Big Sad, you should probably avoid cooking Pasta, Popcorn, and Rice All Together on Toast.* If, like us, the Big Sad means you shove as many carbs as physically possible into your mouth hole, then you're eating, and eating is, as we said earlier, good. This cookbook is a supportive friend, but you're the one living your life. ← *Maybe, like Ash from A+E, your calories come mostly from orange Tic Tacs.*

- In a just society, everyone would be fed. That is, in our opinion, the bare minimum required to call yourself a civilization, so Tories, please take notes. Depending on where you live, you might be able to access some government support, from SNAP to Universal Credit. Beyond this, there are mutual aid organizations, like Food Not Bombs, the Hare Krishnas, Sikh temples, and community gardens.

* We haven't included this recipe in this cookbook because it sounds terrible. If you cook it and it's great, please write in and tell us at nightbeatseu@gmail.com.

It's likely that somewhere near you, there is an organization that believes in feeding people not as charity, but as an act of solidarity. On your bad days, this can keep you fed. On your better days, getting involved in feeding each other is an act of political resistance against a culture hell-bent on crushing you into an isolated, wibbling nub of a human.

★ We wish we could come into all your homes and take care of you. But that's called "breaking and entering" and apparently it's illegal? This cookbook is the closest we could come without "breaking the law" and "committing crimes" and "getting the cops involved."

Eddy, that means you.

Unless they're the fictional werewolf and vampire cops from Night Beats investigating the strength of their feelings, in which case we hope they get as involved as possible.

A note on measurements. Which is to say, note that we haven't put down many measurements. Most of these recipes are flexible enough that you can just kind of wing it, or use ingredients such as a potato that inherently contain measurements, such as one (1) potato. We realize that this system works well for our particular version of the Big Sad, but some people require more structure. To people who share our version of the Big Sad: if cheese makes you feel better, you should add more cheese. Think of ingredients like household cats—if they're helping, you can always add more. To people who don't: if measurements make you feel better, write in some measurements. We're not the boss of you.

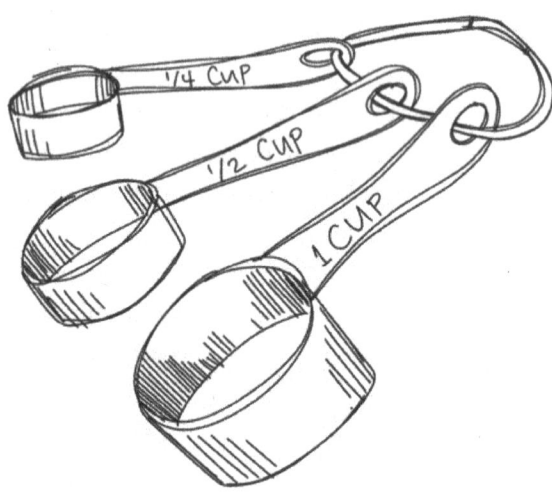

RAMEN VARIATIONS PART 1: CLASSIC RAMEN ⓥ

Sometimes called instant noodles.

Ramen is our ride-or-die. It got us through undergrad, working for poverty wages, and too many depressive episodes to count. It's cheap, versatile, and takes 5–10 minutes to prepare. You can even eat it dry after smashing it up a bit, with the powder sprinkled on top, if cooking seems like it's going to take too many spoons.

Not all ramen is created equal. There are off-brand Mr. Noodles that you can buy three for a dollar, but this is an act of desperation. Consider whether, in fact, you are *that* depressed and/or broke. If you can manage it, Nongshim is substantially pricier but is objectively the best ramen. There are a range of possibilities in between.

> Well, it is subjectively the best ramen, since others also exist. But don't worry, you have a lifetime to select your own favourite.

We recommend swapping up your ingredients so you don't get bored of them.

Core Ingredients
- Pack of ramen, a.k.a. instant noodles
- Boiling water

Preparation I: Stove
- Dump the ingredients in a pot as the water is boiling, then mix it up.

Preparation II: Kettle
- Boil the water in the kettle, add the boiling water, noodles, and flavour package to a bowl, and mix it up.
- Note that the water will be hot enough to cook the noodles but might not defrost any frozen veg that you add. This is why you have a microwave.

- ★ Also note that any measurements on the side of the package are a suggestion, not a rule.

Preparation III: Microwave
- ★ Combine water and ramen in bowl.
- ★ Microwave for 1 min. See if it's cooked.
- ★ If not, microwave another minute.
- ★ Repeat until cooked.

Bottom-Tier Ingredients
These are things you can add that are probably somewhere in your home right now.

- ★ Wilty vegetables. If it's looking sad in the fridge, it will probably taste okay once hot water is added.
- ★ Soy sauce in packets from your last takeout.
- ★ Hot sauce in packets from your last takeout.
- ★ Whatever spices you sweep up from the bottom of your cupboard.
- ★ You can rawdog it from the package if there's nothing else.

Mid-Tier Ingredients
If you add these, it'll taste good, and you likely have at least one.

- ★ Egg*
- ★ The good kind of soy sauce

A note on the humble egg. There are endless ways to add egg to ramen. Hard-boiled, scrambled, or fried—they're all delicious. Look for these recipes in The Humble Egg*.*

There is one egg variation which you can only do with soup, so we're listing it here. Crack the egg into the hot soup, stir it in, and you've got a fair approximation of egg-drop soup. If the water isn't hot enough to cook the egg in the soup, microwave for a minute, stir, and repeat until it is cooked. If you've made the ramen on a pot on the stove, then just keep heating until the egg is cooked.

- ✴ Sriracha
- ✴ Frozen vegetables
- ✴ Fresh vegetables

God-Tier Ingredients

Adding any of these elevates your ramen to next-level shit that tastes like you're a fancy lady who went to a restaurant instead of a sad sack who is crying in front of your TV. We recommend stocking up in between depressive episodes, especially for things that don't go bad.

- ✴ Garlic
- ✴ Onion**
- ✴ Ginger
- ✴ Chilies
- ✴ Kimchi
- ✴ Seaweed
- ✴ Tofu
- ✴ Canned baby corn
- ✴ Sesame oil
- ✴ Hash browns. *Hash browns are delicious in ramen and we don't know why. You have to cook them first before you add them:* see our recipe for French Fries a.k.a. Hot Chips.

**A note on onion preparation. Unless you like raw, crunchy onions, they generally take a little longer to cook than other vegetables, so you should put them in first. The smaller they are, the faster they'll cook, but like some cruel Faustian bargain, the more you'll have to work at chopping them. (Unless you buy pre-chopped, of course.)

That said, ignore any recipe that tells you to cook until translucent or worse, cook until brown. That recipe is not for when you have depression, and they will cook just fine alongside the rest of the ramen as you go.

- ✱ Shiitake mushrooms. These come dried, so you need to rehydrate them. Put them in a jar of water, put that in the fridge, come back to it in a day or three. Chop up the mushrooms. You probably don't want to eat the stem since it will never get soft, but the cap is delicious. The liquid also makes great stock to add flavour to the ramen soup—use it instead of water.
- ✱ You can do this dried mushroom trick with dried seaweed too. Mix them together in the jar.

A word to the wise: Different types of ramen vary as to the vegan-ness, and even vegetarian-ness, of their ingredients. If this matters to you, it's a good idea to check the ingredients closely. Nongshim Soon and Vegetable Mr. Noodles are both vegan.

RAMEN VARIATIONS PART II: INSTANT NOODLES ON A PLATE Ⓥ

Core Ingredients
- Pack of ramen, a.k.a. instant noodles*
- Boiling water

Preparation
- Make your instant noodles with boiling water from the kettle, or by boiling them on the stove like pasta.
- Resist! Do not add the flavour package yet!
- When noodles are soft enough to eat, drain the water.
- Serve on a plate instead of in a bowl.
- Add flavour package to taste. You can always add more, but it's hard to add less. Stir it in.

Mid-Tier Ingredients
- Sauces. You can substitute the flavour package with sweet chili sauce, or anything else you like.
- Basically everything we said was tasty in ramen-as-soup is also tasty in instant-noodles-on-a-plate. *For big stuff like frozen veg or fresh veg, add it to the boiling water. Small stuff like garlic will escape out the strainer when you drain it, so that goes on the plate.*

God-Tier Ingredients
For God-Tier, you're frying some ingredients separately, and thus making a second dish dirty. The oil is necessary for frying success—the rest are all optional to choose between.

---

* *Irish readers, consider making this with koka noodles. We have been informed this is your equivalent to what Canadians call ramen.*

- Oil
- Garlic
- Onion
- Peppers
- Mushrooms
- Frozen veg mix

God-Tier Preparation
- Put some oil in a frying pan. Put on medium heat.
- Loosely chop garlic, and/or half an onion, and/or half a pepper and other tasty things like that.
- Mushrooms are great.
- If you don't want to chop fresh vegetables, you can use frozen veg here.
- Fry the veg in the frying pan. A minute or two?
- Add the cooked noodles and whatever sauce you're using, which might be the flavour package.
- Stir.
- Serve on a plate! Or eat it out of the pan.

RAMEN VARIATIONS PART III: APOCALYPSE RAMEN Ⓥ

This is basically like regular ramen soup but with three critical differences:

* It is intensely chaotic, which is to say that you can pretty much toss anything into it and say you did it on purpose.
* It's slightly healthier, if your depression has lifted enough that you want to eat something other than delicious, delicious chemicals.
* It involves a mason jar, so you can feel like you're riding out the end of days in true hipster style.

Core Ingredients & Supplies
* Mason jar or other heatproof receptacle
* Boiling water
* The only requirement here is rice noodles. Why? Because they cook fast.

Preparation
* Put all ingredients in the jar.
* Boil some water.
* Pour into jar to cover ingredients.
* Shake it up a bit (not right away, otherwise you'll burn your hands and get more depressed).
* Let it sit for a few minutes.
* Enjoy???

Variations

- ✶ Remember those takeout packets of hot sauce and soy sauce? This is a good time to use them.
- ✶ Frozen or fresh vegetables. Wilted is absolutely fine here. *International readers may call them "wilty" vegetables. Reader, you are now bilingual.*
- ✶ Any kind of spices. We particularly suggest garlic or ginger powder, but seriously, anything will work.
- ✶ If you have tofu or some other protein to use, go for it.

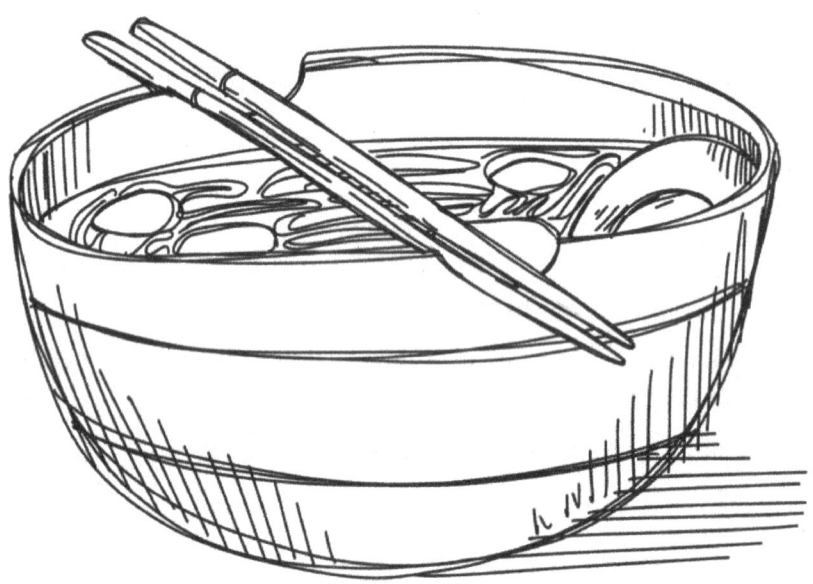

KINDA LIKE PAD THAI Ⓥ

Peanut butter and sweet chili sauce mix together to make something which tastes kinda like you'd imagine Pad Thai sauce would taste if you've never had Pad Thai before. It's delicious. Real Pad Thai is even more so.

Core Ingredients
* Rice noodles
* Boiling water
* Peanut butter
* Sweet chili sauce

Preparation
* Cook the rice noodles. You can cook them like _Pasta_ on the stove, but pay attention. Rice noodles cook much faster than wheat noodles. Alternatively, you can cook them like _Apocalypse Ramen_ in a mason jar and drain the water when they're cooked.
* Add peanut butter and sweet chili sauce to the cooked noodles.
* Stir and eat.
* If the noodles cool down, the sauce might not mix in as well as when they're hot straight out of the boiling water. You could throw the noodles and sauce in the frying pan with a bit of oil.

Variations
* Goes well with a sprinkling of nuts. Peanuts, nut mix, anything really.
* Also good over Italian-style wheat pasta, or other Asian-style noodles, or over instant noodles. See cooking instructions in _Pasta_ or in _Ramen Variations Part II: Instant Noodles on a Plate_, or on the back of the package.
* Defrost and add frozen vegetables.
* Cook and add fresh vegetables.
* Add a cooked egg. Read _The Humble Egg_ for ideas of how to cook it.

PASTA VARIATIONS (V)

Pasta is like ramen noodles but you have to buy the sauce separately. Also, you can't cook them with boiling water straight from the kettle. On the plus side, they come in shapes, and anyone who says that alphabet noodles are only for children is lying.

They even come shaped like penguins, if you know where to look.

Core Ingredients
- Any shape pasta
- Any sauce

Preparation
- Bring water to a boil in a pot.
- Add the pasta to the boiling water.
- You can add salt to the water if it makes you feel like a fancy Italian person with their life together. We're not entirely sure what the salt does.

We are reliably informed that salt makes (most) things better.

- The package tells you how long some corporate chef thinks that shape takes to cook. We're not beholden to their capitalist opinion, also we forget what time we added the pasta anyway. Taste it and make up your own mind. Try not to scald yourself on the water.
- Alternatively, you can tell if it's done by taking out a noodle and flinging it at the wall. If it sticks, you're good. Also, flinging pasta at a wall is a good way to get out your frustrations. *Remember to pick it off the wall later before it becomes a permanent fixture.*
- If you find a stirring spoon at the bottom of your drawer that has a hole in it, the purpose of that hole is to measure out a serving of pasta. The hole is a lie. You can have as much pasta as you want. You can make leftovers for later. You can eat them all in one sitting anyway.
- Keep the water hot. Simmering if possible? Stir occasionally.
- If you have a colander, drain it into a colander. If you're not that posh, use the pot lid or a slotted spoon. *It might seem like a good idea to use a*

plate. *We speak from experience when we say that you will scald yourself and you may break the plate. It is not actually a good idea.*

* Put pasta on a plate or in a bowl. Or back in the original pot to save on dishes.
* Add the pasta sauce out of the jar to the pasta and stir through in a hopeful attempt to warm it.

Variations
We can't imagine adding all these variations to the same bowl of pasta at the same time. Maybe we're just not creative enough.

* A can of crushed tomatoes is technically sauce. It might not have depth and nuance of flavour or a photograph of someone wearing an apron on the front, but that's why God gave us hot sauce and Italian herb mix.
* Olive oil makes great pasta sauce. Surprising but true. Particularly good with other stuff, like salt, or Parmesan cheese, or chili flakes.
* Add cheese. The really cheap powdered Parmesan will survive the apocalypse. We have never seen it go bad. If you've got cheddar cheese, it'll taste better grated than in chunks you pulled off with your fingers, but the nutritional content is the same. You could put cheese singles on instead if you hate yourself.
* Nutritional yeast does some of the things that cheese does if you're vegan or lactose intolerant, and it lasts forever. **If you're on medication—for depression, chronic pain, diabetes, or anything else—check to see if your meds are compatible with nutritional yeast before you eat it.**
* Salsa is basically pasta sauce, use that. *[Then you have the choice of Mild, Medium, Spicy, and, if you can find it, Ruin Your Exit Hole. Choose wisely.]*
* True facts: Many types of canned soup make delicious pasta sauce. Tomato soup & milk & cheddar cheese is highly traditional. So is cream of mushroom soup & a wee bit of milk & crushed up potato chips on top.
* Seeds and nuts. Pumpkin seeds are fully amazing in pasta. So are sunflower seeds, and they're even cheaper. Pine nuts are traditional in pasta, but they're way more expensive than sunflower seeds. Honestly any nut or seed has potential.

THE SAD BASTARD COOKBOOK

- Add raw garlic.
- Add olives. Green or black, from a jar or a can—olives are delicious.
- Hummus also makes an excellent pasta sauce.
- If you're looking for a low-carb alternative, you can buy spaghetti squash and zucchini cut into noodle spirals in the frozen veggies section.

Mid-Tier Pasta Types

- Mix cooked pasta with tomatoes, olive oil, garlic, and black pepper. The goal is to mix things together—only the pasta needs to be actually cooked. You can also add feta cheese if you're not vegan.
- On grocery day, buy some tortellini from the fresh pasta section. Get a nice pesto in a jar instead of the cheapest tomato sauce you can find. You can serve this to a guest and they'll think you put in effort. Which you did.

    Vinny from Sushi and Sea Lions recommends this when you've suffered a crushing financial loss in your unfulfilling career as an emergency services manager for a soul-sucking electric company.

- Honestly any fresh pasta is posh and tastes great.
- Potato gnocchi is a fancy pasta hack. It costs slightly more, and cooks a bit faster, than other types of dried pasta. It stores in your pantry as long as you like, and it tastes good prepared with the same sauces you'd use for anything else. People who don't realise these important gnocchi facts will be impressed when you serve it to them.

    Plus you can start a philosophical debate over whether gnocchi counts as pasta, which is sure to liven up your dinner conversation.

God-Tier Ingredients

If you want to add stuff to the sauce, you're looking at heating it separately before you add it to the noodles, either on the stove or in the microwave. Is it worth it? Only you can decide.

- Add wine. Red goes great in tomato sauce. White goes great if you're using Campbell's cream of mushroom soup as a sauce.

    This is mainly an excuse to open a bottle of wine.

- Add frozen veg. Surprisingly tasty choice: frozen spinach. But only if you can buy frozen spinach as small chunks in a bag. The frozen spinach block takes forever to defrost—you'll give up on eating by the time it's cooked.

* Adding avocado or canned pumpkin to your sauce makes it richer and creamier.
* Add fresh veg. You'll probably have to cut it up. And cook it in the sauce, not just warm it up. I'm not sure this really counts as depression cooking anymore.
* Canned beans, drained and rinsed. Chickpeas are a personal favourite here.

Pro-tip: If you find the Alphagetti in the can a little bland, you can kick it up a notch with your Sriracha.

LITERAL DEPRESSION COOKING

Technically, this recipe came to us from WW2 rationing, not Great Depression-era cooking, but we like puns.

Core Ingredients
* Pasta
* Water
* Cheese
* Ketchup

Preparation
* Cook pasta and drain it.
* Add it back to the saucepan.
* Add ketchup until the pasta doesn't stick to the bottom of the pan.
* Add grated cheese until it is very cheesy.

Variations
* Use canned tomato soup instead of ketchup.

PASTA IN A RICE COOKER Ⓥ

Core Ingredients
* Pasta
* Water
* Sauce

Preparation
* Add equal parts pasta and water to the rice cooker. Maybe a cup of each.
* Push down on the start lever, then lie back in bed.
* When the rice cooker pops to show it is done, dump in some pasta sauce.
* Pick up the rice cooker bowl with a towel, and eat right out of it.

Variations
* Add some shredded cheese if that's your style.

EGGY PASTA

Core Ingredients
* Pasta
* Oil
* Eggs
* Salt

Preparation
* Cook pasta according to the package directions. See *Pasta Variations* for more pasta-related witty banter and maybe some cooking advice.
* Toss the pasta in a frying pan with oil on medium heat.
* Crack eggs over it.
* Stir until cooked.
* Add salt as desired.

Variations
* Pepper would be an excellent addition here.
* Before you add the pasta to the frying pan, chop an onion and fry it in the oil.
* Fry some mushrooms too.
* Add grated cheese.
* Pairs well with ketchup or hot sauce.

PASTA WITH HOMEMADE TOMATO SAUCE ⓥ

This recipe is God-Tier, but it's also very delicious. Make it on a good day, or if you've got guests, or maybe just to treat yourself.

Core Ingredients
- Pasta
- Cherry tomatoes ← *Unless Cam from The Devil You Know ate them all before you could harvest them.*
- Boiling water
- Olive oil
- Salt

Preparation
★ Cook pasta according to the package directions. See *Pasta Variations* for more pasta-related witty banter and maybe some cooking advice. ← *Yes, we copied and pasted that sentence from the previous recipe. Recycling is good for the planet.*

★ Five minutes before pasta is finished cooking, add two handfuls of cherry tomatoes (maybe 6–8 tomatoes) to the boiling water.

★ Drain pasta and tomatoes.

★ Drizzle with olive oil.

★ Add a bit of salt.

★ Stir.

★ Squish tomatoes a little before eating.

PASTA WITH ONE (1) ACTUAL VEGETABLE Ⓥ

This recipe is also God-Tier since it involves cooking both pasta and spinach. We only recommend it because it's tasty.

Core Ingredients

* Pasta
* Spinach (frozen or fresh)*
* Boiling water
* Olive oil
* Cumin powder or cumin seeds (or both)
* Salt

Preparation

* Fry spinach in olive oil and cumin until warm, wilted, and soft. Medium or low heat is all you need. *You can't add too much cumin. There's no such thing. That's just physics.*
* Cook pasta.
* Put spinach on pasta. Add a bit more olive oil and some salt.
* Voila! Spinach over pasta.

Variations

* Add garlic or onions or whatever to the spinach when you fry it.
* Use zucchini instead of spinach.

---

* If you buy fresh spinach, make sure that it comes pre-washed in the bag. Washing spinach is far too much effort. If you buy frozen, get the kind that comes in chunks not in a giant block. Defrosting the giant block takes an annoyingly long time.

* Or radish greens instead of spinach. They're basically identical except for being cheaper.
* You could do other stuff with the fried spinach too! Serve it over rice. Add it to quesadillas. Chuck it in ramen. Hide it in your enemy's shoes. Spinach fried with cumin has countless uses.

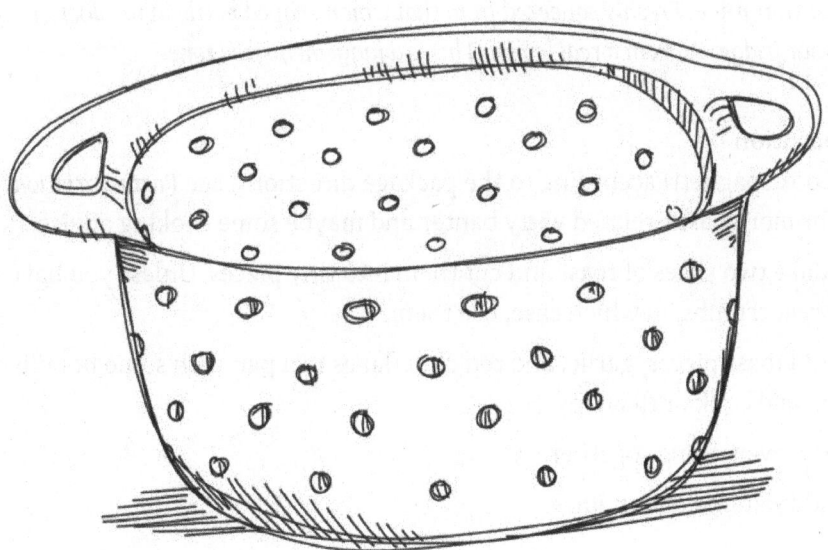

SPAGHETTI AGLIO E OLIO Ⓥ

Again, God-Tier effort and God-Tier tastiness.

You can tell because the recipe's name is in Italian.

Core Ingredients
* Bread or breadcrumbs
* Spaghetti
* Olive oil
* Red chili flakes and salt
* Garlic (fresh chopped, frozen, from a jar, or garlic salt)
* Lemon juice. *Freshly squeezed from that lemon shaped bottle in the door of your fridge. Or from a real lemon. This is a judgement-free zone.*

The first edition of the cookbook forgot this ingredient. Oops! Sorry, Italian readers!

Preparation
* Cook spaghetti according to the package directions. See *Pasta Variations* for more pasta-related witty banter and maybe some cooking advice.
* Make two slices of toast and cut them into tiny pieces. Unless you have breadcrumbs, in which case, use them.
* Add toast pieces, garlic, and red chili flakes to a pan with some hot olive oil and cook until crispy.
* Mix everything together.
* Add salt and lemon juice.

MAC & CHEESE

Most Canadians will tell you that macaroni and cheese is the ultimate comfort food. We call it mac and cheese for short, or Kraft Dinner, shortened to KD, even when we don't buy the Kraft-branded box. Other countries have boxed pasta and cheese, and sometimes it's even branded as Kraft Dinner. But it doesn't taste the same as the Canadian version. KD might be the only thing this colonialist country got right.

Core Ingredients
- Box of store-bought mac & cheese
- Milk
- Butter

Preparation
- Boil water on stove
- Add the pasta from the box. The result will be less sad if you stir it at least once.
- When the pasta is cooked, drain the water.
- Add milk and butter to the pot. Don't measure. Add the package of strangely orange cheese powder to the pot. Add the noodles back to the pot. Stir. *All of this can be done in any order.*
- Stir some more.
- If the butter isn't melting, you can turn the burner back on low to melt the butter.
- If you added far too much milk, that's okay. Cheese soup with pasta is great too.
- You can eat this from the pot, or you can put it in a bowl, or even on a plate.

Variations

You can do anything with mac and cheese. It's magic.

- Add ketchup.
- Or salsa.
- Or garlic powder.
- Or fresh garlic.
- Or broccoli.
- Or hummus.
- A splash of soy sauce is a surprisingly good addition.
- People will look at you funny if you add honey, but it has been known to happen.
- Live your best life.

RICE VARIATIONS PART I: COOK THE RICE (V)

There are lots of types of white rice, like long-grain, parboiled, basmati, etc. Buy whatever type is the intersection of the Venn diagram of "cheapest" and "I like best." All white rice (besides instant rice) cooks more or less the same way.

There are other ways to make rice, but if you're at the point of exploring that particular rabbit hole, you might not need this book anymore.

Core Ingredients
- White rice. *Instant or regular, depending on how you want to cook it.*
- Water

Preparation I: Instant Rice
Instant rice is God's gift to depressed people who don't have rice cookers or don't want to clean one afterwards. It comes in different varieties and tastes more or less as good as most other rice but takes half as long. It's also impossible to burn, for those of us with a tendency to forget what we put on the stove.

Different types of instant rice will have different instructions, but the method is basically the same.

- Boil water. Let's assume you do this in a pot on the stove. You will end up using equal parts rice and water, so if you don't have a measuring cup, you can use a glass or a mug to measure.
- When your water is boiled, put the boiling water and the rice together in the pot. Cover for as long as it says on the box (usually 5 minutes or so). Fluff up the rice with a fork, or whatever utensil you have available, or if you're in full goblin mode, a stick you found on the ground.

* If you boiled the water in the kettle, there's no point in getting a pot dirty just to combine the boiling water and rice. Put the rice in a bowl with a plate for a lid. You can eat it out of that same bowl for added efficiency.

Preparation II: Rice Cooker
Rice cookers are great when you are too tired or depressed to stand over the stove. If you have a person in your life who struggles with depression but likes rice, and it's getting close to their birthday, we seriously suggest a rice cooker as a gift. Maybe that person is you, and you buy it for yourself. Rice cookers are magical devices that make nice food while you're back in bed.

The fancy rice cookers with lots of buttons are nice, but the cheap ones with only one button do the job plenty well.

* Wash your rice cooker, because you probably skipped the final step of these instructions last time.
* Add equal parts white rice and water.
* You can add a little extra water if you like it moister.
* Put on the lid.
* Click the start button.
* Come back when it makes the happy "rice is ready!" noise.
* Or not, rice cookers always have a "keep warm" function so it's fine if you miss the noise.
* The easiest way to clean the rice cooker is to pull out the inner pot, fill it with water, and let it soak. Wash it in the morning. Or right before you use it next.
* If you're not gonna wash the rice cooker, leave it open so it dries out instead of staying moist and getting moldy.

Preparation III: Rice on the Stove
* Add rice (maybe 1 cup?).
* Add twice as much water as rice (maybe 2 cups?).
* Cook on high heat, without stirring, until the water reaches the top of the rice.

FOOD YOU CAN MAKE SO YOU DON'T DIE

- ✹ Cover the rice with the lid and turn off the stove.
- ✹ Leave the pot on the stove (with the heat off) for ten minutes or so.
- ✹ Come back and there's rice!
- ✹ Word to the wise: It's easier to cook rice if you make at least one cup of dried rice. If you try to make less, it's likely to burn. But the more the merrier—leftover rice is really useful. Just keep it in the fridge between meals.

Variations

- ✹ You can eat it as is. Plain rice can be really comforting when you're feeling a bit nauseous.
- ✹ You can add sauce. Literally any sauce. Soy sauce, salad dressing, hummus, pasta sauce, hot sauce.
- ✹ You can also add lots of other stuff. We have more rice variations waiting for you in the next few pages.

You can even add chocolate sauce, if you're not a coward. Personally, we are cowards.

Brown rice exists but we're not sure why. Wild rice is amazing but we're scared in case it cooks differently—it might require paying attention.

RICE VARIATIONS PART II: ADD STUFF TO THE COOKING WATER

If you add flavouring to the cooking water, the rice absorbs it as it cooks. Boom! Flavoured rice! These can go with either instant or regular rice.

Core Ingredients
* Dried rice, instant or regular, which you can cook with flavourings and vegetables and stuff.

Variations: Flavouring
Add a stock cube or some spices to the water before it cooks. We recommend mushroom stock or curry powder. If you're only making a wee bit of rice, you can add only part of the stock cube, but rice makes great leftovers.

* The saddest variation: Add a stock cube to the rice-water mixture and stir a bit. It won't fully dissolve right away, but you can even out the flavour by stirring some more once the rice is done cooking.
* More effort and less sad variation: Boil water in the kettle, dissolve the stock cube in a mug of hot water and add it to the rice. Then add the rest of the water as usual.
* Saffron is popular and adds a really nice colour.

Variations: Vegetables
This is an ideal place to use frozen or wilty vegetables, since they cook with the rice. For God-Tier, make regular rice on the stove or rice cooker, wait until it's partway done, then throw the vegetables on top of the rice to steam. For us mere mortals, add them at the beginning so you don't forget. If you do this with instant rice, you might need to microwave it at the end if the veggies aren't fully cooked.

* Add any frozen vegetables. Peas are a classic.

- ✱ Or any wilty vegetables from the back of your fridge.
- ✱ Or fresh vegetables, if you've got them and are willing to chop.
- ✱ Add canned beans. Drain and rinse them, of course. Rinsing in the can totally works and saves washing the colander. If you add them now, they will get warm with the rice. If you add them after cooking the rice, they'll be closer to room temperature. The choice is yours.

God-Tier: Coconut Rice

If you're replacing the water with something—for example coconut milk—you need to make rice in a pot or a rice cooker. Boiling coconut milk in the kettle to make instant rice sounds like an idea with negative long-term consequences to the kettle.

- ✱ Replace half the water with coconut milk. Cook as usual.
- ✱ Goes great with some frozen veg thrown in before cooking, and some seeds or nuts added after cooking.
- ✱ You can also cook rice normally, add some of a can of coconut milk, a little curry powder, and sweet chili sauce for a delicious take on Thai coconut curry!

RICE VARIATIONS PART III: ADD STUFF TO THE COOKED RICE Ⓥ

These can be made with fresh rice, or leftover rice you heat up in the microwave.

Core Ingredients
- Rice (see Rice Variations Part I & Part II for cooking instructions and flavouring ideas)

Variations: Flavouring
It's hard to know what to say here. Rice goes with most sauces. Whatever you have in the cupboard or fridge will probably taste good. Here are some classics to start you off.

- Soy sauce
- Sesame oil (combines well with soy sauce)
- Any bottle of stir fry sauce. Teriyaki. Hoisin. Black bean. Anything. Mix and match.
- Laoganma chili oil
- Canned soup
- Any jar of curry sauce. Korma. Vindaloo.
- Salsa
- Hummus
- Scoop in some butter or margarine with a fork. Bonus: you can then eat the rice straight out of the cooker with that buttery fork.

Note that vindaloo is spicy, and is not for the weak of mouth like Zilla. It may need extra chilis in it for spice fiends like Rachel.

Variations: Stuff
- Frozen vegetables. Defrost your vegetables of choice in the microwave and add.

- ★ Canned beans. As always, drained and rinsed. *We talk about this in* <u>Bean Salad</u>. *Skip ahead. Break the rules.*
- ★ Canned vegetables.
- ★ Chinese preserved vegetables.
- ★ Nuts and seeds.

Mid-Tier Variations
- ★ Fresh vegetables, raw. Chunks of fresh tomatoes are really tasty mixed with rice, olive oil, and sea salt. Canned chickpeas would be good here too.
- ★ Fresh vegetables, cooked. Whatever is in the fridge or pantry. Chop some zucchini or carrots, put them in a bowl with a little water in the bottom and microwave them. Or fry some mushrooms and onions.
- ★ A humble egg. See <u>The Humble Egg</u> for cooking instructions for fried, scrambled, and hard-boiled. Any of these go well with rice.
- ★ Cheese.

Hot tip: You can mix and match from these rice variations! Add nuts to the top of instant rice you cooked with a stock cube. Go wild, you beautiful rebel!

ANOTHER RICE VARIATION: BLACK BEANS & RICE (V)

This is probably two or three meals for one person, and it reheats well. It doesn't require much use of hands, or lifting anything heavy, because that's a shape of disability accommodation we sometimes need.

Core Ingredients
- Rice
- Canned black beans
- Spices as desired
- Salsa or tomato paste or hummus

Preparation
- Make rice or use already made leftover rice. If it's not hot, microwave it.
- Drain and rinse a can of black beans.
- Put the beans in a microwave-safe bowl.
- Add any spice or seasoning mix you have handy to the beans. *We like smoked paprika, garlic powder, salt, and/or black pepper, but you can use anything from oregano to a chili seasoning mix.*
- Microwave the beans until they're as hot as you like (a couple of minutes, probably).
- Mix the rice and beans.
- You can add salsa, any kind you have around, or a bit of tomato paste, or hummus. *Try the kind of tomato paste that comes in tubes—it's perfect when you only want a little.*
- Stir and eat.

God-Tier: Almost Like Rice and Peas

Authentic rice and peas are a staple of Jamaican cuisine and taste amazing. This is not that.

* Instead of canned black beans, use kidney beans.
* Instead of water to cook the rice, use coconut milk. (See *Rice Variations Part II* for an in-depth description of making rice with coconut milk.)
* Add scallions, thyme, allspice, and scotch bonnet pepper or sauce.

RICE VARIATIONS PART IV: FRIED RICE (V)

This is our favourite thing to do with leftover rice. It's so delicious and easy that sometimes we'll cook fresh rice just so we can make fried rice. But the true genius of this recipe is turning leftovers into a solid meal.

Core Ingredients
* Cooked rice, hot or cold
* Oil

Preparation
* Add oil to the frying pan.
* Turn on to medium heat.
* If you have fresh or frozen vegetables, add them now and fry them. Stir sometimes so everything cooks and nothing burns. Ideally don't overfill the pan now—you want to leave room for the rice.
* Add the rice to the frying pan.
* Add more oil. This ain't health food.
* Stir occasionally so all the rice has a chance to fry.
* If you want to add sauce, now is the time to pour it on the rice and stir it through.
* Eat!

Variations
All the flavouring and vegetables stuff we suggested you could add to rice in _Rice Variations Part II_ & _Part III_ are good here too. Instead of repeating ourselves, here's a few things which are specifically good on fried rice.

* You really want some kind of sauce on this. If you've got any soy sauce around, put it on.

- Our personal favourite fried rice sauce is soy sauce and sesame oil.
- Garlic and onions. Add these during the vegetable step. You can buy pre-chopped.
- Fresh or frozen vegetables. Sliced mushrooms are amazing here.
- Tofu chunks. Add during the vegetable step so you can fry them. Firm tofu preferred.
- Egg. There's a special egg variation only available to fried rice. Here's the secret. After you add the rice, crack an egg on top. Stir it through as you stir the rice. The egg will coat the rice grains, giving the fried rice a lovely eggy flavour.
- Spices as seasonings. You can add these during the vegetable step or during the sauce step. We do it during the sauce step because we're bad at estimating how much spice we'll want until we see it on the rice. Curry powder is a personal favourite.

FRIED NOODLES Ⓥ

You make these exactly like you make _Fried Rice_, but using noodles. Some people call them "Greasy Noodles" which gives you an idea how much oil these noodles can take.

Core Ingredients
* Cooked noodles, hot or cold
* Oil

This is almost exactly the Fried Rice preparation but with "rice" replaced by "noodles." Look, we promised easy, not creative.

Preparation
* Add oil to the frying pan.
* Turn on to medium heat.
* If you have fresh or frozen vegetables, add them now and fry them. Stir sometimes so everything cooks and nothing burns. Ideally don't overfill the pan now—you want to leave room for the noodles. _Watch your arms and for the love of all things edible, don't do this shirtless._
* Add the noodles to the frying pan.
* Add more oil. This isn't health food. Another glug or two. Or three.
* Stir occasionally so all the noodles have a chance to fry.
* If you want to add sauce, now is the time to pour it on the noodles and stir it through.
* Eat!

Variations
Literally do the things we told you to do with _Fried Rice_. The only difference is that you've got to pick a type of noodle to use. Decisions are hard, so we recommend getting a d6 dice, assigning a number to each type of noodle you have in the house, and rolling for it.

- ★ Udon noodles can be used straight out of the package without cooking them first.
- ★ Rice noodles can be cooked using only hot water from the kettle—see the instructions in _Apocalypse Ramen_ or _Kinda Like Pad Thai_.
- ★ You could take the noodles out of a pack of instant noodles and use those. See cooking instructions in _Ramen Variations_ or _Instant Noodles on a Plate_.
- ★ Any Asian-style noodle will be amazing, but mostly you'll need to cook them on the stove with boiling water. There'll be instructions on the back of the package.
- ★ Italian-style wheat noodles will work in a pinch.

Send noods instead of nudes. Mail these to your friends. Fried noodles spark joy.

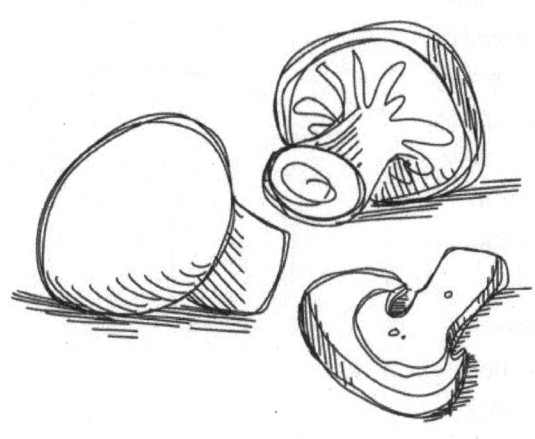

COUSCOUS VARIATIONS Ⓥ

You can think of couscous like instant rice or instant noodles that come in a different shape. You can make it with only a kettle, a bowl, and a spoon. It tastes good with lots of different sauces and lots of different additions. Most of the things that go well with rice or noodles will also taste good with couscous. Our personal favourite is to add Moroccan-style flavourings.

Core Ingredients
- Couscous
- Boiling water

Preparation
- Boil the kettle.
- Put some couscous in a bowl.
- Add boiling water until it just covers the couscous + maybe 1 millimetre.

  If you're bad at measurement and/or American, a millimetre is the smallest unit of measurement that you can actually see.

- Cover the bowl, maybe. *You can cover the bowl in cling wrap to keep the heat in, if you can find the end of the cling wrap on the roll. Sounds unlikely. Put a plate on the top instead, if you've got a clean plate. Fuck it. Don't put anything on it. It'll cook well enough.*
- Wait until the water looks like it's absorbed, then fluff it with a fork.
- Consume.

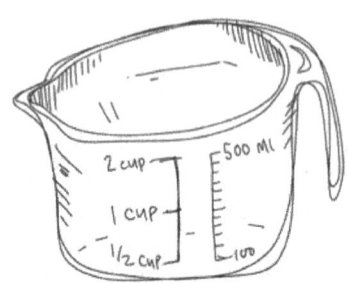

Mid-Tier: Moroccan Style

Add some or all of these ingredients, depending on what's in your kitchen. Spices can be added before or after cooking.

* Dried raisins
* Dried nuts
* Hard-boiled eggs
* Salt
* Spices: cinnamon powder, cumin powder, ginger powder.
* Scoop some hummus on top.

POTATO VARIATIONS
PART I: BAKED Ⓥ

Potatoes are proof that evolution was a good idea. They're the ideal food. You can boil them, bake them, fry them, or turn them into vodka. Just ask Samwise Gamgee from The Lord of the Rings.

Peeling potatoes is time consuming and dramatically lowers the nutritional content of the potato. Lots of really nutritious stuff is just below the peel. We only mention this in case someone tells you that they prefer eating mashed potatoes without bits of peel. It's more socially acceptable to talk about nutrition than it is to explain about depression coping mechanisms. It shouldn't be—we should live in a world where mental illness can be discussed openly. But some days it's easier to talk about nutrition than to be the change, and picking your battles is a life skill for an activist.

If you don't peel the potatoes—and why would you—make sure you wash off any dirt. Dirt has a terrible texture. Ideally, buy washed potatoes. This is the only problem that capitalism can solve for you.

Core Ingredients
* Potato

Preparation I: Baked Potato in the Oven
Known as a jacket potato in the UK.

* Turn on the oven at 350°F or 175°C or so. Precision is for suckers.
* Put the potato in the oven for three years or until slightly squishy when you poke it with a fork. *Rohan, author and professional chef, tells us it takes about an hour, depending on potato size. Experience tells us that it always takes longer than you think.* [Do not put your potato in the oven for three years.]
* Take the potato out of the oven.

- Cut the potato in half and add toppings to both sides. *We suggest you use oven mitts or a tea towel or a regular towel to avoid burning your hands.*
- If you cook extra potatoes, then you'll have leftovers you can heat up in the microwave later, or eat cold, or turn into *Bubble and Squeak*. Adding more potatoes to the oven doesn't increase the cooking time.
- Baked potato hack: Before putting your potato in the oven, rub it all over with oil and salt. It will make the skin taste like a big delicious potato chip.

Preparation II: Baked Potato in the Microwave
- Poke the skin of the potato a few times with a fork. This is necessary so the steam can escape. If you don't, the steam will explode out of the skin and coat the inside of the microwave with potato. Also, poking potatoes with a fork is cathartic.
- Microwave until squishy when you poke it with a fork. The internet says 7–10 minutes but it'll depend on your specific microwave. It will also take longer than you think.
- Cut the potato in half and add toppings to both sides.
- Putting more than one potato in the microwave at once will increase the cooking time.

Variations
You can top a baked potato with anything. Classics include:

- Margarine or butter
- Salsa
- Peanut butter
- Baked beans
- Hummus
- Cheese (cheddar, feta, American pseudo-cheese slices . . .)
- Red onion
- Sour cream (yogurt also works)
- Tears (of your enemies?)

POTATO VARIATIONS
PART II: BOILED Ⓥ

Core Ingredients
* Potato

Preparation I: Boiled Potatoes on the Stove
* You could boil a whole potato, but it will take a really long time.
* It's much faster if you chop the potato into chunks.
* Boil the chunks in a pot of water on the stove until squishy.
* Top as described in *Potato Variations Part I: "Baked."*

Preparation II: Russian Construction-Worker Potatoes
This is a microwave version of boiled potatoes. It is named in honour of the man who taught it to us.

* Cut potato into chunks.
* Put potato chunks in a bowl with a wee bit of water (like a tablespoon or two) at the bottom of the bowl).
* Microwave until edible. Probably the same 7–10 minutes range.
* Add salt.
* Add butter or margarine.
* Stir and eat.

POTATO VARIATIONS
PART III: MASHED (V)

Core Ingredients
* Potato

Preparation: Mashed Potatoes
* Boil potato chunks or microwave them in a bowl with a wee bit of water.
* Cook until they are extremely squishable, not just regular squishy.
* Squish with fork or with fancy potato masher or with even fancier potato ricer.

Variations
You probably shouldn't add all of these at the same time.

* Add milk, plant milk, or a bit of the water you boiled the potatoes in and mix through.
* Add margarine or butter and mix through.
* Add yogurt and mix through.
* Add chives and mix through.
* Add baked beans on top.

God-Tier: Kinda Like Skordalia
* Take cold mashed potatoes.
* Add cut-up raw garlic.
* Add lemon juice.
* Add olive oil.
* Mix.
* Optional: add yogurt and ground almonds.

POTATO VARIATIONS
PART IV: FRENCH FRIES

Also known as "hot chips."

Speaking as younger Gen Xers and older Millennials, all we know is eat hot chip and lie.

Core Ingredients
* Potatoes, washed, OR
* Any type of frozen-potato-substance (fries, hash browns, tater tots, waffle fries a.k.a. potato waffles, etc.), OR
* Sweet potatoes
* Oil. *If you're in Canada, probably canola oil. We're not sure what other countries use for their generic cheap vegetable oil.*
* Salt

Preparation I: Starting with Raw Potatoes or Sweet Potatoes
* Consider your life choices. Raw potatoes are much cheaper than frozen, and they store for a long time in the dark (for example, in the fridge or in the pantry). But they take much longer to cook. And you need to chop them up yourself.
* Okay, so you're going with raw?
* Wash and chop potatoes. *If you chop them into cubes, call them "home fries." If you chop them into longbois, call them "French fries." Or "hot chips" in Ireland.*

Preparation II: Starting with Frozen-Potato-Substance
* Dig the half-full bag of store-brand French fries out from the bottom of your freezer.

Yes, you have half a bag. Trust us, it's there.

Variation: Fries in a Frying Pan
You need to stand near the frying pan as it cooks, and pay some attention. If you don't stir occasionally, the bottom of the fries will burn before the tops cook at all.

- Add oil to the frying pan. Several glugs. And add more during cooking if the pan looks low. You want enough oil that the bottom of all the potatoes are in oil, but not enough to cover their tops, because that would be deep frying and that's not *Sad Bastard* level.
- Add chopped potatoes or whatever frozen-potato-substance you have.
- Cook on medium.
- Stir occasionally. You want to leave it still long enough to get crispy, but not long enough that the bottom turns to charcoal and the fire alarm goes off.
- When it achieves desired crispiness levels, turn off the stove and put the fries on a plate.
- Add salt and enjoy.

Variation: Fries in the Oven
- Put the chopped raw or frozen-potato-substance in a pan or on a baking sheet with raised edges.
- Pour a bit of oil over the potatoes. Use your hand to mix the oil and the potatoes on the pan so they all get some.
- Bake at 350°F or 175°C.
- Halfway through cooking, take them out of the oven and stir so both sides get cooked. *If you're cooking a frozen-potato-substance, it might give you a time on the bag. Otherwise, it's probably about 20–25 minutes, so check on them after every ten minutes or so and give them a stir. Set a timer so you don't forget and end up with burnt fries.*
- When they have reached the desired crispiness level, salt and eat.

Variation: Fries in the Microwave

These are not, strictly speaking, good. But they're a step up from eating French fries still frozen straight out of the bag.

- Put frozen-potato-substance on a plate.
- Microwave until no longer frozen.
- You're going to want to add more salt than that to make up for the texture.

FRENCH FRY VARIATIONS: NOW WHAT? Ⓥ

So you've got fries, or hash brown, or tater tots. Now you're ready to take dinner to the next level.

Core Ingredients
* Cooked fries or other potato-type-substances
* Courage

Variations: Spice
When you're adding the salt, you can add spices too.

* Try seasoning salt instead of plain salt.
* Smoked paprika
* Chipotle powder

Variations: Dip in Sauce
* Ketchup
* Mayonnaise
* Ketchup and mayonnaise mixed together
* Sriracha hot sauce
* Sriracha mixed with mayonnaise
* Sriracha mixed with honey
* Tartar sauce, which is mostly relish mixed with mayonnaise.
* Mushroom gravy heated in the microwave
* Hummus

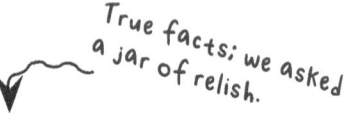
True facts; we asked a jar of relish.

Variations: Put Stuff on Top
* Vinegar. Malt or white vinegar are traditional.

- ✱ Microwave baked beans from a can and pour them on top.
- ✱ Put shredded cheddar cheese on top. Or other cheese.
- ✱ Fry an egg and put it on top. See _The Humble Egg_ for cooking advice.
- ✱ Fried mushrooms and onions. These pair well with mushroom gravy from a tin.

> Our lawyers advise that we remind you to take them out of the can before you microwave them.

Stuff on Top of Fries Variations: Not-Poutine & Not-Disco Fries
- ✱ Microwave mushroom gravy from a can.
- ✱ Cheese. Cheese curds if you want to call this "poutine," and American cheese slices if you want to call this "disco fries."

Stuff on Top of Fries Variations: Not-Potatas Bravas
- ✱ Tomato-based pasta sauce
- ✱ Jalapenos from the jar
- ✱ Cheese

Stuff on Top of Fries Variations: Not-chos
- ✱ Black beans or refried beans, heated in the microwave.
- ✱ Salsa
- ✱ Cheese

Bottom-Tier: Chip Butty
This is a British delicacy. It's known as a chip sandwich in Ireland. We hope you enjoy your international cuisine.

- ✱ Put fries between two slices of buttered bread, or in a bun.

Mid-Tier: Potato Waffles with Eggs
These can be made with any type of frozen potato substance, but they're traditional with potato waffles (a.k.a. waffle fries).

- ✱ Fry two potato waffles in the frying pan with a little oil until cooked. You want enough oil so all of the bottom of the waffle is touching oil, but not so much that it covers the top of the waffle. Anything in the middle is good. You'll need to flip them partway through cooking so both sides get crispy without the bottom side turning to charcoal. *If they turn black and your fire alarm goes off, you left them too long. We've all been there, and we are sorry for your potato loss. You can make a new batch or eat something else.*

* Break the egg on top of the waffles and spread around so the egg goes into the holes.
* Flip over.
* Season with salt and pepper.

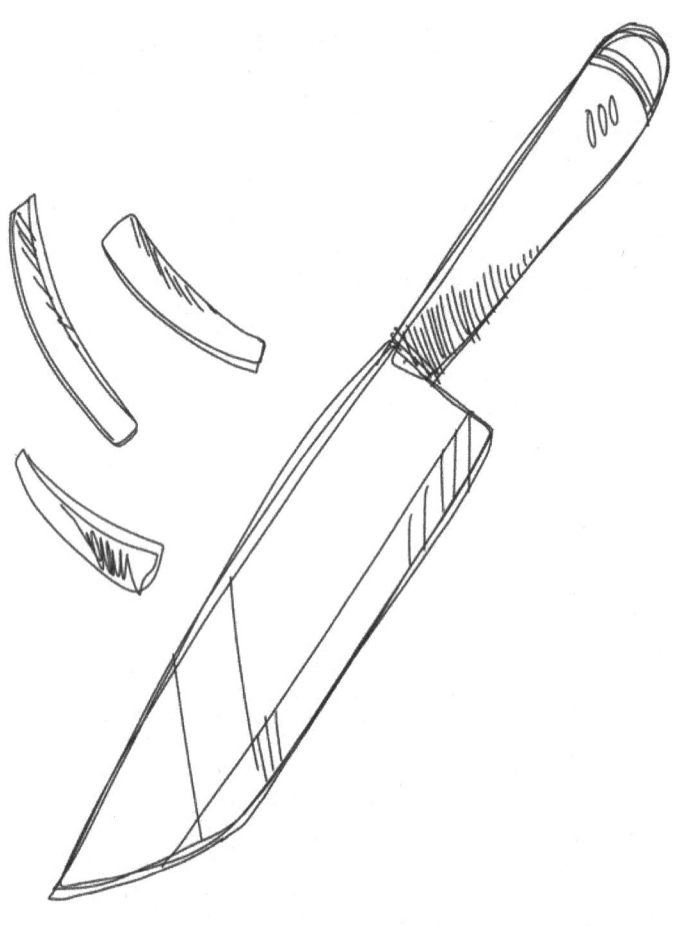

SPRING ROLLS Ⓥ

If you find spring rolls in the fridge section, or marketed as appetizers for parties, they're usually kinda expensive. But we've found frozen vegetarian spring rolls which are pretty cheap—sometimes in specialty Asian grocery stores but sometimes at the local grocery store. The secret is to buy the cheap frozen vegetarian spring rolls even if the box claims you need to deep fry them. You don't need to. We promise.

Cooking instructions are basically the same as making frozen *French Fries* from a bag.

Core Ingredients
* Frozen spring rolls
* Oil

Preparation I: Spring Rolls in a Frying Pan
You need to stand near the frying pan as it cooks and pay some attention. If you don't stir occasionally, the bottom of the spring rolls will burn before the tops cook at all.

* Add oil to the frying pan.
* Add spring rolls to the frying pan.
* Cook on low or medium.
* Occasionally flip the spring rolls so both sides get crispy. It takes about 10 minutes.
* When it achieves desired crispiness levels, turn off the stove and put the spring rolls on a plate.

Preparation II: Spring Rolls in the Oven
* Put the spring rolls in a pan or on a baking sheet with raised edges.
* Pour a bit of oil over the spring rolls. Use your hand to mix the oil and

the spring rolls on the pan so they all get some.

- Bake spring rolls at 350°F or 175°C.
- Halfway through cooking, take them out of the oven and stir so both sides get cooked. *It'll probably take 15-25ish minutes to cook them, so maybe flip at the 10 minute mark? Set a timer so you don't forget.*
- When they have reached the desired crispiness level, eat.

Preparation III: Spring Rolls in the Microwave

They will not get crunchy in the microwave, but they will get hot, and they contain the same nutrients regardless.

- Put spring rolls on a plate.
- Microwave until no longer frozen.

Spring rolls are delicious on their own, or with a dipping sauce. Plum sauce is a classic. They also pair well with *Fried Rice*.

*A UK-based recipe tester informed us that the brand Tiger Tiger: Tsingtao Spring Rolls *are both cheap and delicious. In their oven, those spring rolls took 25 minutes to cook from frozen. Unfortunately, as their oven is, and we quote, "pretty terrible," we have no idea what temperature they cooked at. Extrapolate at your peril.*

HANGOVER BUBBLE AND SQUEAK (V)

Rachel learned this recipe from a roommate following a night of unhealthy imbibing. Upon looking it up, it turns out that Bubble and Squeak is an actual British dish and not something said roommate just made up to mess with her. This is a lazy version of that, designed to use up leftovers in your fridge before they go bad. Remember those baked potatoes you made the other day? Here's what you do with any that you have left.

Core Ingredients

* Potato (These should be already cooked. You can use any remnants of the <u>Baked Potato</u> recipe.)
* Cooking oil or butter
* Salt and pepper
* The rest of your leftovers

Preparation

* Put oil or melt butter in a frying pan on medium heat. If you're using onions, let them get a head start with the frying.
* Mash up the potatoes with a fork or the edge of your spatula if they're not already mashed.
* Dump in the potatoes and any other ingredients and fry for about 10 minutes. Keep pressing everything down with your spatula or whatever you have.
* Flip it over and add some salt and pepper. Fry for another few minutes. You're aiming for golden brown but we'll settle for not burnt.
* If you're using an egg, drop it in right at the end to quickly fry.

Mid-Tier

* Chopped onions
* Fried egg
* Any chopped vegetables. You can use frozen vegetables as well but it'll take a bit longer.
* Some British people will tell you that *Bubble and Squeak* needs to include

cabbage, spinach, or some other green. They can think that. We have nothing against the British people, only their fascist governments.

God-Tier

* The God-Tier version of fried potato bits is called latkes, which you should look up and make when you're feeling better.

Marah from Query will be proud.

ROASTED VEGETABLES (V)

Core Ingredients
* Vegetables that can be roasted. *Root vegetables work particularly well! We recommend potatoes, carrots, parsnips, squash, celery root, onions (red tastes best but yellow is cheapest) and sweet potato.*
* Cooking oil
* Salt

Preparation
* Cut vegetables to roughly the same size. They can be basically any size, but we recommend about the size of your thumb. *Though thumbs can also be any size.*
* Put cut vegetables on the baking sheet.
* Pour some oil on.
* Sprinkle some salt on.
* Mix it around with a spoon or your hand so they all get some oil.
* Put in the oven at 350°F or 175°C.
* Cook for 20 minutes. *Set a timer so they don't burn while you're back in bed.*
* If it doesn't seem done, give them another 10 minutes, and check again.

Variations: Vegetables
* Potatoes
* Sweet potatoes
* Vegetarian sausages. *These are technically not vegetables, but they are often made from vegetables.*
* Bell peppers
* Broccoli
* Canned beans. Chickpeas or fava are great here.
* Cherry tomatoes

Make sure you remove them from the can. Do not roast the can.

- Brussels sprouts
- Eggplant
- Zucchini
- Cauliflower

Variations: Other
- Add spices along with the salt.
- Serve on cooked _Pasta_.
- Put a fried egg (recipe from _The Humble Egg_) on top.
- Crumble some feta cheese on top. Other cheeses work too.
- Use a dollop of hummus as a dipping sauce.

PANCAKES (V)

Big Pancake doesn't want you to know this, but making pancakes is easier than you think. There are dozens of recipes, and we couldn't agree on the best one, so we're including a bunch of them. Pick whichever you can make with the ingredients you've already got in the kitchen.

Remember that time is an illusion, lunchtime doubly so, and you can eat pancakes for any meal.

Core Ingredients
* Cooking oil or butter or margarine
* Flour
* Water
* Eggs or baking powder or yeast & sugar (depends on the recipe)

Preparation I: Irish-Style Pancake Batter
These make a flatter pancake than American-style fluffy pancakes. A more refined, European pancake. Something heading in the direction of a crepe, but not closing the distance.

These pancakes are as flat as the spaceship that crashed into the asteroid in Alinda.

We include weights, since that's how the recipe was contributed, but if you don't have a scale you could try 1 cup of flour and 1 cup of water. If you want it thinner, add more water. If you want it thicker, add more flour. *Write the quantities you like best in the margins. Personalize this book.*

* Mix together:
    > Flour (100 g)
    > Water (300 g a.k.a. 300 mL)
    > 1 raw egg
    until they turn into pancake batter.

Preparation II: "Two of Everything" Fluffy Pancakes

* Mix together:
  - Flour (2 cups)
  - Water (2 cups)
  - Baking powder (2 teaspoons)
  - 2 raw eggs

  until they turn into pancake batter.

* Let it sit for a few minutes for the baking powder to do its thing. *Make yourself a cup of coffee.*

Preparation III: "Even Fluffier" Fluffy Pancakes (Can be Veganized)

* Mix together:
  - Flour (2 cups)
  - Water (1.5 cups)
  - Baking powder (3 teaspoons)
  - 2 raw eggs (optional)
  - Dollop of vegetable oil

  until they turn into pancake batter.

* Let it sit for a few minutes for the baking powder to do its thing. *Make yourself a cup of tea.*

* You might need to play around with the amount of liquid—add a bit more if it's too thick. You can always add more flour if it ends up too liquidy. *Repeat this process forever to end up with infinite pancake batter.*

Preparation IV: Vegan Pancakes with Yeast

These are a bit more complicated, but we didn't want to leave vegans out of the pancake adventures. The previous recipe can be veganized deliciously, but this one doesn't even call for eggs.

* Mix together:
  - Dry instant yeast (2 teaspoons)
  - Sugar (2 teaspoons)
  - Room temperature water* (2 cups)

---

* Yeast will grow best in slightly warm water. They'll grow a bit slower in cold water, but they'll get there in the end. Boiling water will kill them, and then they can't work their yeasty magic.

- ✱ Let it sit for a few minutes for the yeast to do its thing. *Make yourself a cup of hot chocolate.*
- ✱ Add flour (2 cups).
- ✱ Mix until it turns into pancake batter.

Preparation V: Pancake Mix from a Box

If you're dealing with something like depression, pre-mixed ingredients can be a gift. They're more expensive than the individual ingredients. Our society makes it financially costly to be physically or mentally unwell because it doesn't consider human life to be intrinsically valuable. We have opinions on our society.

If you do buy boxed mix, we highly recommend getting the version where all you add is water and butter. If you're adding eggs and milk, you might be paying four times as much for flour in a box. Don't waste your money on the Pancake Industrial Complex.

- ✱ Mix together:
    - ▸ Whatever the box suggests until it turns into pancake batter.

Preparation: Do This No Matter What

- ✱ Turn on medium heat and let the pan warm up a bit. Or not, if you're hungry and rushing.
- ✱ Add cooking oil to the frying pan.
- ✱ Add a scoop of batter to the hot frying pan. Some people use a ladle. We use the cup measure we got dirty when measuring the flour. Save yourself washing the ladle.
- ✱ You wanna cook the pancake some of the way through so it's got structural integrity, then flip it and cook the bottom. How do you know when it's time to flip? Crepe-style enthusiasts tell us to swirl the pancake batter around the pan, flip, and serve. Fluffy-pancake connoisseurs speak of waiting for bubbles to appear in the pancake, then flipping and waiting a minute or two. Personally, we adopt a "trial and error" approach.**

** *For whatever reason, the first couple of pancakes never turn out as well as the later ones. To paraphrase a famous chef, "The pan needs to get to know the pancakes, and the pancakes need to get to know the pan."*

Variations: Batter

Enhance your pancake experience by adding these.

* If you substitute milk or plant milk for the water, you'll get a richer pancake. This only works if you have milk in the house, which sounds unlikely.
* Add frozen fruit to the pancake batter. Don't defrost it first.
* Add fresh fruit to the pancake batter. *If you add fresh blueberries to the pancake batter, they will turn into weapons-grade pockets of molten juice. You have been warned.*
* Add a pinch of salt to the batter.
* Add 3 tablespoons of sugar to the batter.
* Add a dollop of vanilla. Or two.

Variations: Toppings

* Peasant: lemon and sugar
* Layperson: nutella
* Gymfreak: peanut butter and strawberry jam
* Tennis player: sliced strawberries and cream
* Canadian: maple syrup
* British: golden syrup
* Spiced: cinnamon and sugar
* Loaded: yogurt, nuts and defrosted frozen fruit
* Dutch-style: cheese and apple slices
* Savoury: hummus, fried mushrooms, and spinach fried with cumin. Maybe with a fried egg on top?
* Any or all of the above. Maybe not all at once.

KOREAN-INSPIRED PANCAKES Ⓥ

We have it on good authority that saying "inspired by" is how you get away with dubious claims. Unfortunately, eating these pancakes will not magically transport you to South Korea. They taste pretty okay, though.

Core Ingredients
* Pancake batter ingredients. Select your variation of choice from *Pancakes*. Ideally the batter would be made with water instead of milk, but if you're using a mix that has milk, that's okay.
* Cooking oil
* Green onions (sometimes called spring onions or scallions). We imagine this works with regular onions up chopped really small, but we've never tried, because no one can be bothered to chop onions that small.
* Soy sauce

Preparation
* Make pancake batter. *We're so old we remember when these were called 1337 h4x.*
* Cut up the onion. *Elite hacks: Cut up green vegetables and herbs with scissors instead of a knife. It's faster and easier. It works on green onions, but it also works on nappa cabbage—anything green and thin.*
* Add the onion to the batter.
* Add cooking oil to the frying pan. Turn on medium heat.
* Add a scoop of batter to the hot frying pan. Some people use a ladle. We use the cup measure we got dirty when measuring the flour. Save yourself washing the ladle.
* Flip when it's partway cooked and cook a bit longer. *See previous recipe for when to flip.*
* Serve with soy sauce for dipping.

Variations

* Add other veg as well as onion. You can add anything, but you need to cut it up small enough to stay inside the pancake instead of instantly falling out. Napa cabbage is already flat, so it's a great one. *Cut it with scissors.* Zucchini and mushroom are both very tasty if you can be bothered to slice them thin.
* Vary your dipping sauce. For example, instead of soy sauce on a plate, you could put Sriracha on a plate. Or both! *On the same plate!*
* The Saddest Bastard: if you don't have onion, or don't like onion, omit it and just use some other veg.

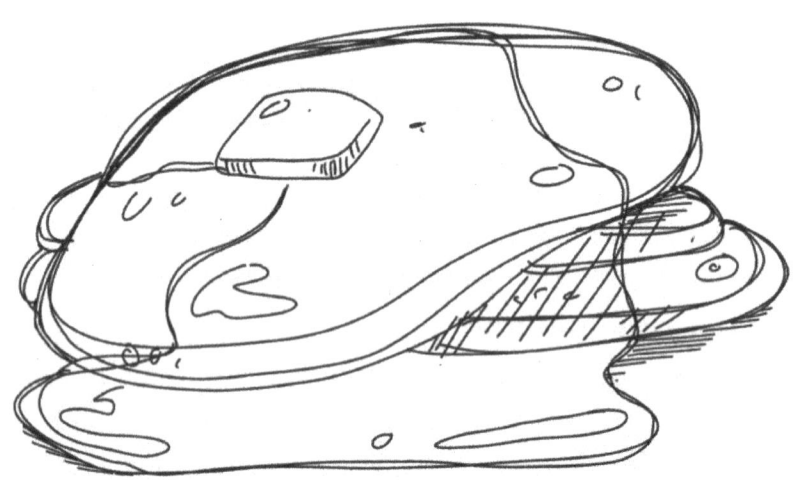

OATMEAL VARIATIONS (V)

Core Ingredients
* Instant oatmeal
* Boiling water

Preparation
* Take a single-serving package of instant oatmeal. Realistically, take two of them at once.
* Pour into a bowl.
* Pour boiling water over the oatmeal.
* Wait?
* Stir.
* Enjoy?

Mid-Tier Preparation
* You can buy a full bag of instant oatmeal, you don't have to buy it in single-serve packs.
* You have to add your own flavourings and measure out servings.
* But it's much cheaper.
* And you don't have to measure very well, just eyeball it.

Variations
Add some or all of these to cooked oatmeal.

* Milk or plant-milk
* Yogurt (or plant-yogurt)
* Candy
* Peanut butter
* Nuts

- * Seeds
- * Dried fruit
- * Fresh fruit
- * Cinnamon powder
- * Sugar
- * Honey
- * Maple syrup
- * Jam

THE HUMBLE EGG

An egg is a versatile thing. These egg recipes can be main meals. They can be snacks between meals. You can add them to other meals, like ramen, toast, and couscous. You probably shouldn't eat them raw, Disney movies notwithstanding, but luckily eggs are easy to cook.

If you get eggshell in your egg, you can fish it out with a spoon, or with the spoon-shaped half an eggshell that's already in your hand. It won't kill you if you eat it, so no need to panic. *Unless there's hidden treasure involved like in Birds of Fortune, in which case, go ahead and panic about eggs.*

Core Ingredients
* Egg(s)

Preparation I: Hard-boiled Eggs
There are as many different ways to boil an egg as there are grandmothers to teach us how to do it. This one involves paying the least attention.

* Add water to a pot. At a minimum, you want the water to be the height of the egg, so the egg can float. More water is okay, but too much water and it'll take a long time to boil. We're not made of patience.
* Optional: add salt to water.
* Bring water to a boil.
* Add eggs.
* Put lid on pot to keep the heat in.
* Turn off the stove.
* Wait 30 minutes. *Longer is fine. Go watch an episode of a TV show and come back. Go ahead and finish the whole season. The egg can wait.*

- The egg is boiled!
- If you've made extra eggs for later, good job! Go you!*

Preparation II: Scrambled Eggs & Omelettes In the Microwave

- Crack eggs into a microwave-safe container. Use the plastic tupperware that your Chinese takeout came in, or take a microwave-safe mug and spray the inside with cooking oil.
- Stir with fork, making sure to break the yolks.
- Add salt and maybe pepper. Stir through.
- For omelettes: Cook in the microwave for a minute or so. Check if they're done. If not, cook for another 30 seconds, and repeat until they're solid.
- For scrambled eggs: do the same thing, but every 30ish seconds take it out of the microwave and stir it with the fork.

Preparation III: Fried or Scrambled Eggs & Omelettes On the Stove

- Put some oil, butter, or margarine in a frying pan.
- Turn on the stove to medium heat.
- Crack the egg into the frying pan.
- Leave the egg alone until most or all of the clear liquid has turned into a white solid.
- If you take it out now, that's called "sunny side up."
- If you flip it over and don't break the yolk, so it's still a yellow liquid, that's called "over easy."
- If you break the yolk at any point, or you cook the yolk to a yellow solid, that's okay! That's how you make eggs "over hard." That is a valid cooking option.
- If you stir the eggs a bunch, that's "scrambled eggs."
- If you stir the eggs in a bowl, then pour them in the pan and don't touch them again until they're cooked through, that's an "omelette."

If you don't peel the leftover eggs immediately (and why would you?), make sure you've got a method to tell cooked and raw eggs apart in the fridge. Drawing smiley faces on the shell works wonders.

God-Tier

* Cook in onions and tomatoes.
* Add cheddar cheese. At any stage. Mix some chunks in before you microwave. Grate it on after it's cooked. Don't make us admit you can do this with cheese singles. But you can.
* Serve with salsa.
* Serve with ketchup.
* Serve with soy sauce. Probably not at the same time as salsa and ketchup.
* Add ready-made hollandaise or those little hollandaise packets. Some wilted spinach makes it a cheater's Eggs Benedict. Hollandaise sauce is not traditionally served on an omelette, but no one can stop you.

If, like Takuma from Melancholic Parables, you only eat food with a name that begins with a vowel, an omelette might be the dish for you.

CHINESE-STYLE EGGS & TOMATO

Core Ingredients
- Eggs
- Chopped tomatoes
- Chopped garlic
- Salt
- Oil
- Rice

Preparation
- Add oil to a fry pan and turn it to low or medium heat.
- Add chopped garlic to the fry pan.
- Add eggs to the fry pan and stir them around so they become scrambled eggs.
- Add chopped tomatoes to fry pan and stir around so they get a bit soft.
- Add salt. More than a pinch.
- Serve over rice.

Variations
- Add soy sauce. Soy sauce is salty, so taste test before you add infinite salt and infinite soy sauce to the same dish.
- Add sesame oil.
- Add Shaoxing wine.

EGGS & BREAD VARIATIONS

Core Ingredients
* Eggs
* Bread

Preparation I: Eggs on Toast
* Toast bread
* Cook <u>The Humble Egg</u>—fried, scrambled, or hard-boiled. If it's hard-boiled, you can slice it or mash it with a fork.
* Goes well with mayonnaise, butter, margarine, or ketchup.

Preparation II: Eggs in a Hole
* Cut out a hole in the middle of the bread. *Snack on the cut-out bread while doing the rest of the steps.*
* Put a bit of oil or butter in a frying pan on medium heat. Put the bread in the frying pan.
* Crack an egg into the hole. Cook it until the clear liquid starts going white where it touches the pan.
* Flip the toast so the egg cooks on both sides. If you flip it too soon and some of the whites aren't cooked, you can always flip it back. *[We assume this is how it got the name.]*
* Congratulations! You have an egg in a toast hole.
* Optional: add salt and pepper.

Preparation III: French Toast, or, Eggy Bread
* Crack egg into a shallow bowl (*or a deep bowl if the shallow ones are all dirty*). Break the yolk with a fork and mix it around a bit.
* Add a splash of milk if you're feeling fancy. Mix that in with the fork.
* Dip bread into the egg mixture. Flip so both sides get eggy.

- Place in a frying pan with a little butter or margarine or oil. Fry on medium or low just until golden on both sides.
- Can be served with lots of toppings, including: jam, maple syrup, golden syrup, honey, dried fruit, defrosted frozen fruit, fresh fruit, nuts, cinnamon, and/or yogurt. Anything that tasted good on *Pancakes* will taste good on French toast.

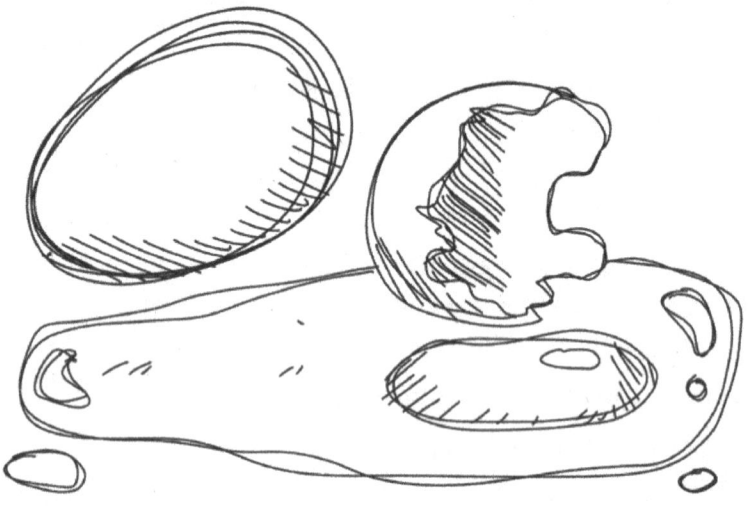

BEAN SALAD Ⓥ

The idea that bean salad is difficult to make is a lie perpetuated by Big Bean to keep you in their thrall.

Core Ingredients
* Canned beans. A bean medley is preferred. We've used anything from a four-bean mix up to an eight-bean mix.
* Salad dressing. Probably Italian dressing.

Preparation
* Open the can.
* Drain and rinse. You can rinse it in the can. Or in a colander if you're posh enough to wash the extra dish. Two extra dishes, since you can't add salad dressing to a colander.
* Optional: put the beans in a bowl.
* Add store-bought salad dressing of choice.

You can eat it from the can, but you are legally obligated to say, "Fine like this," as you do.

Mid-Tier
* Prepare it in a large bowl and serve it on a plate.
* Defrost some frozen veg in the microwave and add it. Frozen corn is a personal favourite.
* Canned corn also tastes great.
* You can use olive oil and vinegar instead of store-bought dressing. Yes, it's two ingredients instead of one, but it's two ingredients that never go bad.

God-Tier: Approach with Caution
* Chop up actual fresh vegetables and add them. Onion, particularly red onion, is traditional in bean salad. So is celery.

We cannot recommend raw celery under any circumstances, but we've heard some people like it.

LENTILS IN A POT Ⓥ

Core Ingredients
- Canned lentils (this makes good leftovers, so consider making two cans if your pot has space).
- Water
- Salt

Preparation
- Drain the liquid from the can.
- Rinse the lentils, probably in the can. *Lentils are wee and some of them will escape. It's okay.*
- Pour the lentils into the pot. Add maybe a can of water for every can of lentils. If you want it thicker, add less water. If you want it more soup-like, add more.
- Cook on medium heat, stirring occasionally so the lentils on the bottom don't burn. Add more water if it gets thicker than you want it to be.
- If you add a lot of water and cook it just long enough to heat it, congratulations, you've made lentil soup!
- If you add less water and cook it until the lentils get really mushy, good job on your lentil stew.
- Add salt, more than you think you need. ← Trust us.

Variations
- This also works with chickpeas instead of lentils.
- Lentils also come dried—you'll need more water and much more time if you want to do it this way, though.
- Salt is great, but what about adding other spices too? Like pepper and curry powder? Or chili flakes? If you can get a hold of berbere, a fantastic Ethiopian and Eritrean spice mix, it works really well for this.
- Add a can of crushed tomatoes. Or some tomato paste from a tube.

- ★ Add garlic and onions when you add the lentils. You can get these pre-chopped and frozen.
- ★ Fresh garlic hack: Throw three or four garlic cloves into the water with the beans. Let them cook alongside the beans. Fish them out of the soup, and squeeze them out of their peels by hand. Stir the delicious garlic paste into the soup.
- ★ Add frozen vegetables with the lentils. Frozen spinach is excellent here.
- ★ Fresh vegetables need to cook for a bit longer, but they'll be a tasty addition.
- ★ Add root vegetables if you can commit to standing beside the stove until they cook. Chop some potatoes, carrots, or sweet potatoes. You have to wash them but you don't have to peel them.
- ★ Serve over _Rice_ or _Couscous_.

CHEATER CHANA MASALA (V)

Core Ingredients
* 1 jar tikka masala sauce
* 1 can chickpeas

Preparation
* Drain and rinse canned chickpeas.
* Pour into a pot with the jar of tikka masala sauce.
* Simmer until thickened.

Variations
* Slice in tomatoes, peppers, or potatoes if you have the spoons for veg.
* Serve over _Rice_ or _Couscous_.

Mid-Tier
* Pre-made sauce can be expensive. A can of chopped tomatoes with some spices is usually much cheaper. We recommend adding a lot of curry powder, a pinch of salt, and a pinch of sugar.

CAN OF SOUP (V)

Core Ingredients
* Can of soup
* Sometimes the side of the can tells you a type of liquid to combine with the soup

Preparation
* Check on the side of the soup can to see if you add liquid.
* Open soup can.
* If you don't need to add anything, pour the soup in the bowl until that bowl is full.
* If you need to add liquid, don't fill the bowl more than halfway with the canned soup. Then add the liquid and stir. *Don't measure.*
* Put the bowl in the microwave for 1-minute intervals until hot.
* If you stir every minute, you are less likely to end up with soup all over the inside of your microwave.

Variations
You can add basically anything at this point:
* Cooked rice, couscous, or pasta. *See our recipes for these:* Rice, Couscous, *and* Pasta.
* Seeds
* Canned chickpeas or other canned beans. Drained and rinsed, please.
* Hot sauce
* Specific flavours of soup will taste better with certain additions than others, but it's all the same in your stomach. Don't be afraid to experiment.
* Cook Pierogi and add them to the soup.

* A friend once served Zilla canned lentil soup but he drizzled olive oil over the soup in the bowl and then topped it with a few leaves of fresh parsley and she legit thought he'd made it from scratch.

Bottom-Tier: Even Less Complicated

We often eat soup from the can without bothering to heat it up. We don't even open the can the whole way. That way, it has two hinges and opens like the Skydome and you're Godzilla with a spoon.

* Eat cold out of the can.

Rachel notes that it hasn't been called the Skydome for 20 years. She also notes that she will continue to call it the Skydome regardless.

DUMPLINGS (V)

Frozen dumplings are excessively delicious. If you're lucky, you can get tasty and cheap ones at your local grocery store. If not, stock up next time you're at a specialty Asian grocery store. They come in all kinds of varieties, as nearly every culture on Earth thought up the brilliant idea of taking tasty things and wrapping them in dough.

Core Ingredients
* Frozen dumplings

Preparation I: Boiled
* Boil water in a pot.
* Add frozen dumplings.
* Cook for the length of time it says on the bag.
* Drain and serve.

Preparation II: Pan-Fried
* Check the bag to see if there are any instructions about this. *Pro-tip: You can save yourself some cooking time by microwaving them a bit before frying.*
* Pour some oil into the pan and heat the pan on medium. *No, more oil than that.*
* Fry dumplings until golden brown at the bottom, swirling the pan around a few times.

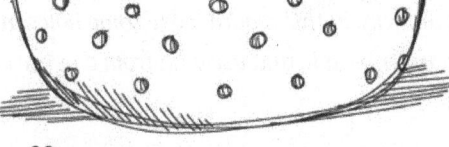

God-Tier: Steamed Dumplings

Steamed dumplings are one of those things that look like they'd be hard to make but if you happen to have a steamer*, they're actually faster than boiling. Frozen dumplings will stick to the bottom of the steamer, so use a piece of parchment paper (poke some holes in it first) and save yourself the washing up.

* Select a pot or pan which is the right size for the steamer to sit on top.
* Add water to that pot or pan, and heat it until it's boiling. You want enough water that it can boil for ten-ish minutes without all the water boiling away.
* Put the steamer on top.
* Put the lid on the steamer.
* Leave it there until the dumplings are tasty. There might be suggested cooking times on the side of the bag.

Variations

* A dipping sauce can be nice. Soy sauce is a classic.
* Dumplings make a great addition to other meals to bulk them out and add variety. Serve with _Rice_ or _Fried Rice_, or with _Fried Noodles_ or _Instant Noodles on a Plate_. Or put them in your _Ramen_ soup!

---

* _Bamboo steamers are amazing, but not everyone is lucky enough to have one. If you're unlucky in this regard, poke some holes in parchment paper and line the inside of a colander with it, and use a lid from a pot to cover it. It's kinda the same thing. Kinda._

PIEROGI Ⓥ

These are tasty potato-filled packages. The freshly made ones are heavenly, but even the frozen ones are pretty damn good. Hopefully they're for sale in the freezer section of your local grocery store. If not, find a specialty international grocery store which carries Polish food and stock up.

They cook exactly like dumplings, even though they taste different.

Core Ingredients
* Frozen pierogi

In the interests of laziness, we're cutting and pasting the prep instructions. The Variations are totally different though, we promise. Well, mostly different. Look, writing a cookbook is harder than you'd think, and none of us majored in Cookbook Writing.

Preparation I: Boiled
* Boil water in a pot.
* Add frozen pierogi.
* Cook for the length of time it says on the bag.
* Drain and serve.

Preparation II: Pan-Fried
* Check the bag to see if there are any instructions about this. *Pro-tip: You can save yourself some cooking time by microwaving them a bit before frying.*
* Pour some oil into the pan and heat the pan on medium. *No, more oil than that.*
* Fry the pierogi until golden brown at the bottom, swirling the pan around a few times.

Variations
* If you add cheese when you fry them, they will get deliciously cheesy.
* Serve with sauerkraut and/or chopped pickles.
* Serve with yogurt or sour cream. Yogurt is basically the same as sour cream and you can use it for more things later. Like *Parfait*.

- Add pierogi to _Canned Soup_ to bulk it up.
- If you have a Ukrainian Church nearby, they might sell homemade pierogi, which are one of the best things you've ever eaten. Blueberry pierogi changed Zilla's life.

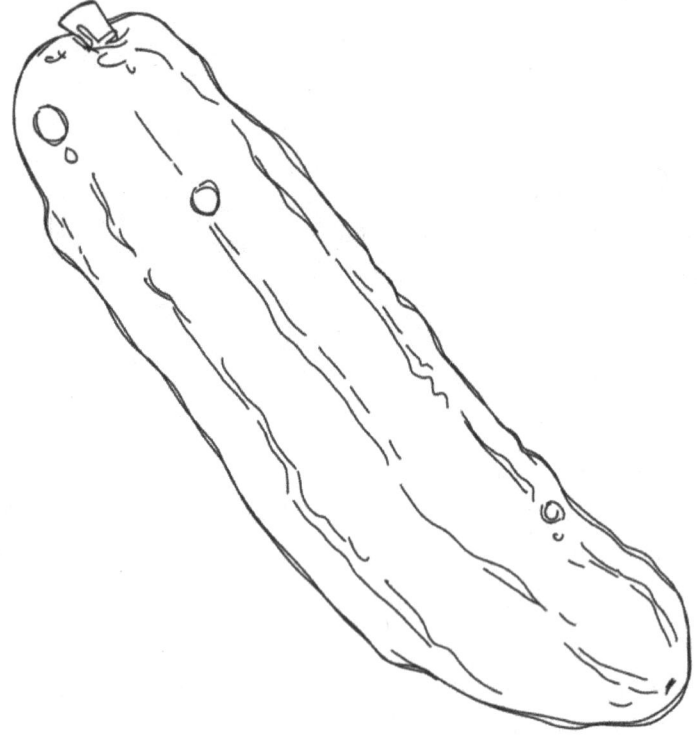

PEANUT BUTTER ON A SPOON Ⓥ

Core Ingredients
* Nut butter. *Peanut butter is the cheapest nut butter, but it's good to have alternatives if you're allergic or your workplace has a peanut butter ban.*

Preparation
* Eat directly out of the jar, on a spoon.

Variations
* Works equally well with other nut butters. *Peanut, almond, Wowbutter, whatever you like can be substituted in all of these.*
* You can also do this with hummus.
* Mix together one-to-one nut butter to honey (or maple syrup if you're Canadian/vegan). Eat.

Non-Spoon Variations
* Spread on crackers.
* Spread on hard pretzels.
* Spread on soft pretzels.
* Spread on cheddar cheese slices.
* Spread on apple slices.
* Spread on bread, optionally with jam.

This is also a good exhaustion food when you need to ingest some energy in order to recharge enough to manage more cognitively-demanding meal prep.

PEANUT BUTTER BALLS (V)

Make semi-portable, extra-high protein snacks! This requires arm strength or cleaning a blender or a food processor. And it requires more preparation than literally eating out of the jar. But you can make it on a good day and freeze it so that you have food for bad days.

Core Ingredients
- An amount of nut butter (depending on how many balls you want).
- A slightly lesser amount of honey, maple syrup, date syrup or other syrup-y thing, or an equivalent amount of brown sugar.
- Some bit of protein powder or almond flour or what-have-you.

Preparation
- Stir by hand or with a food processor or a blender.
- Shape into a ball.
- Optional: freeze so they stay in ball shape.
- Consume.

Variations
- Use canned chickpeas instead of protein powder, but you'll need mechanical assistance to stir this, and who wants to wash the food processor? *Rachel A. Rosen, that's who.*
- Add oats for superior structural integrity.
- Add chocolate powder.
- Add chocolate chips.

APPLE SLICES YES (V)

Core Ingredients
* Apples

By popular demand, we are including apple slices as its own recipe instead of as a recipe variation. The people have spoken.

Preparation
* Quarters is the fewest number of cuts you can make and still easily remove the core.
* You can cut it into more pieces if you want to.
* If you're only gonna cut the apple into halves, you might as well just eat the whole apple as is.
* If you're lucky enough to have an apple corer/slicer device, you basically won the apple-eating lottery.

Variations
* Spread with peanut butter in the ratio most appealing to you and consume. Or use a spoon or melon baller to scoop the seeds out and stuff the peanut butter in where they were—if you do this, you can get away with only cutting the apple into halves.
* Cheese has an added slicing step, unless you buy the pre-sliced packs, which some people do.
* Either of those could also be combined with crackers.
* Sprinkle cinnamon on top.
* Other sliceable fruits, such as pears or peaches, can be enjoyed in similar manners.

This cooking instruction is surprisingly controversial. Some people say that spreading the peanut butter on each slice is a waste of effort, when you could put a dollop of peanut butter on a plate and dip the slices in. Others respond that dipping in solid peanut butter works about as well as dipping apple slices in solid cement. This is going to be a bigger fight than what colour that one dress was, or whether capitalism has any role in a just society.

Preparation

✶ Don't eat grapefruit if you're on SSRIs.

✶ Same with blood pressure meds.

EAT A DILL PICKLE OUT OF THE JAR WHILE STANDING IN FRONT OF THE FRIDGE Ⓥ

Core Ingredients
* Dill pickle

Preparation
* Eat a dill pickle out of the jar while standing in front of the fridge.

Variations
* Eat over the sink to catch drips.
* Eat some shredded cheese instead.
* Maybe some hunks of cheddar that you tore off the cheese block.
* Or some olives from the jar.
* Fruit? Do you have some blueberries in the fridge? Grapes?
* Vegetables? Maybe a cherry tomato?
* Did you remember to leave any _Peanut Butter Balls_ in the freezer?
* There must be something in the fridge you can eat.
* You can't stand in front of the open fridge for the rest of your life.
* Maybe you *can*, but you *shouldn't*.

POPCORN (V)

Core Ingredients
* Popcorn

Preparation I: Microwave
* Microwave the bag of popcorn for 15 seconds less than it says to on the bag, or it'll burn.

This depends on your microwave. Rachel's requires 10 seconds more.

Preparation II: Air Popper
* Start by owning an air popper.
* Add popcorn kernels and turn on.
* You can eat the plain popcorn that comes out.

Variations
* You can melt some butter or margarine in the microwave and put that on top of plain popcorn.
* You can use the spray oil you bought for cooking as a way to add oil.
* Oil or butter or margarine will make other stuff stick, so now you can add salt.
* You can add spices like smoked paprika.
* Or buy cheese powder from Bulk Barn and add that.

EDDY NO (V)

Core ingredients
* Any kind of cereal

Preparation
* Eat, dry, out of the box.

Mid-Tier
* Pour into a bowl, add plant milk. Plant milk comes in cartons, which means it doesn't go bad in your pantry like weak-ass cow milk.
* Or add yogurt instead.
* Or yogurt and jam!
* Maybe some fruit on top? Fresh or frozen and defrosted in the microwave?
* Or nuts, dried fruits (like raisins, cranberries, and blueberries), and seeds (like sunflower seeds).
* If you use a can of fruit and pour in the juice, you don't need milk or yogurt.

Eddy-No-Tier
* Pour into a bowl, and add cream-based liquor of your choice.

CHIPS (V)

Core ingredients
- Chips

Preparation
- Same as cereal, but with a bag.
- Only difference: Do not pour chips into a bowl with milk. Not even with oat milk.

Variations
- Rachel has a bowl shaped like a skull and feels less depressed when she can eat chips out of that, pretending she's eating from the skull of an enemy.
- Dip into salsa. Traditionally done with nacho chips, but we're not cowards. Any chip will do.
- Dip into refried beans from a can. You can heat them up first in the microwave if you want to.
- Dip into guacamole. Buy it from a store, or our recipe for *College Guacamole* is a delicious and not especially complicated version to make.
- Dip into hummus.
- Chip sandwich. *Or, in Ireland, a crisps sandwich!* Spread butter or margarine on two slices of bread, put chips in between, and enjoy.
- Chip sandwich, but this time with peanut butter instead of butter.

Zilla believes that chips in a skull bowl are an ideal dish to serve at your affinity group's potluck. They provide much needed fuel and saltiness when you're gearing up for civil disobedience or navigating an in-group love rhombus. Read Query to find out other things Zilla would do under those circumstances.

COLLEGE GUACAMOLE (V)

You can buy guacamole premade from the store. Or buy an avocado and a jar of salsa and do this.

Core Ingredients
- Avocado
- Salsa

Preparation
- Scoop the contents of avocado minus the seed into a bowl.
- Pour in salsa from a jar.
- Mash with a fork.
- Eat with chips or with a fucking spoon.

THE FASTEST NACHOS

Core Ingredients
You can make this vegan by using salsa instead of cheese as your core ingredient

* Tortilla chips, a.k.a. nacho chips
* Cheese or salsa (or both)

Preparation
* Spread some tortilla chips on a plate.
* Dump shredded cheese on the tortilla chips. If you didn't buy pre-shredded cheese, tear off chunks of cheddar like a Palaeolithic human tearing rocks off a mountain.
* Alternatively, pour salsa on the chips.
* Stick that plate of chips in the microwave like the high-class delicacy it is.
* After 30 seconds or a minute, take them out of the microwave and eat them.

God-Tier
Same thing but in the oven instead of in the microwave.

Variations: Add on Top Before Cooking
* Corn, canned or frozen. If you're using canned, drain them. Rinse them too, if you're feeling fancy. If you're using frozen, defrost them in the microwave.
* Sliced olives
* Canned jalapeno slices
* Other canned chilis, if you're the kind of wild rebel who doesn't think jalapenos are hot enough.
* Cut up raw onion, if you're into that.

Variations: For Dipping After Cooking
* Salsa
* Canned refried beans, put in a bowl and heated in the microwave
* Yogurt or sour cream
* Hummus

Mid-Tier: Not a Burrito
* Put some canned refried beans in a bowl and heat them in the microwave.
* Put the warm refried beans on a plate.
* Add any other ingredients you want.
* Crush some tortilla chips and put them on top.
* Eat with a fork.

QUESADILLAS & PUMPKI-DILLAS
PART I: THE BASICS (V)

If you're vegan, you probably don't want to make the cheese version. Check out the _Pumpki-dilla_ Variation instead.

When it comes to the type of wrap you use, we're not purists. If the "wrap" in the bread aisle is cheaper than the "tortilla," use that.

Core Ingredients
- Tortilla or other wrap-like food substance
- Oil
- Cheese, probably cheddar, probably shredded, AND/OR,
- Canned pumpkin, AND/OR,
- Sweet potato

Preparation: Quesadilla
- Take a tortilla, sprinkle half of it generously with grated cheese, fold over.
- Put a bit of oil in a frying pan and heat on medium.
- Cook on both sides in the frying pan until a little bit browned and the cheese is melted.
- Or microwave the quesadilla for 30 seconds.

Preparation: Pumpki-dilla
Canned pumpkin or mashed sweet potatoes make an incredible filling, and they hold the quesadilla together even without cheese. If you're vegetarian, you can add this to your regular quesadilla, but it's a great alternative for vegans.

- Take a tortilla, spread canned pumpkin on one side, fold over.
- Put a bit of oil in a frying pan and heat on medium.

- Cook on both sides in the frying pan until a little bit browned.
- Or microwave the pumpki-dilla for 30 seconds.

Variation: Boiled Sweet Potato
- Wash the sweet potato.
- Chop the sweet potato into chunks so it boils faster. *Alternatively, buy the pre-chopped sweet potato—a little pricier, but it'll save you effort.*
- Boil until squishy.
- Mash with a fork. You can take off the skin at this point but why bother.
- Apply like canned pumpkin.

Variation: Microwaved Sweet Potato
- Wash the sweet potato.
- Pierce the sweet potato skin with a fork a few times so the sweet potato doesn't explode in the microwave.
- Microwave 7–10 minutes or so, until squishy.
- Scoop out the insides with whatever not-completely-filthy utensil is closest at hand. *You can eat the skin, but it gets a weird texture in the microwave.*
- Apply like canned pumpkin.

Pro-tip: Wraps don't freeze particularly well—they stick together in the freezer, tear when you defrost them, and thus become unwrappable. If you've got leftovers to use up, the Wraps recipes are perfect for you.

QUESADILLAS & PUMPKI-DILLAS
PART II: VARIATIONS Ⓥ

Core Ingredients
* A quesadilla or pumpki-dilla (see previous recipe)

Variations: Dip it in Sauce
Sauce is so good with a quesadilla that we almost made this part of the core recipe.

* Salsa
* Guacamole, either from the store or make *College Guacamole*.
* Sour cream or yogurt.
* Sour cream or yogurt that you've mixed with spices. We recommend some of these: salt, garlic powder, onion powder, cumin, paprika, chili powder, cayenne.
* Hummus

Variations: Add Stuff Inside the Quesadilla
* Black beans out of a can
* Refried beans scooped out of a can and spread onto the tortilla.
* Avocado slices
* Thawed frozen corn or drained canned corn
* Fried diced onion
* Fried green pepper
* Fried garlic
* Fried or microwaved zucchini pieces
* Spinach fried with cumin powder

WRAPS (V)

Almost any leftovers can be turned into a wrap, and you've magically created a different meal than you ate for the last four days.

Core Ingredients
* Tortillas or wraps, whatever was cheapest
* Anything at all to put inside

Preparation I: Wrapped Up

Though we advise against soup.

You can roll just about anything into a wrap. Classics include:

* Yesterday's leftovers.
* Rice
* Couscous
* Roasted vegetables
* Cooked French fries.
* Canned beans
* Refried beans from a can.
* Baked beans from a can.
* *The Humble Egg*, **prepared in any style.**
* Cheese
* Lettuce
* Chopped tomatoes
* Salsa
* Spices
* Sauces
* Some or all of the above mixed together.

Preparation II: The Spiral

Any spreads which are good on _Toast Variations_ are good on wraps. If you put a line of hummus down the centre of the wrap and then add bulky items like lettuce and rice, you can roll it into a wrap. But what if all you want in your wrap *is* the spread? Fear not, brave Reader! Spread it all over one side of the wrap, then roll it into a spiral.

- Hummus
- Butter or margarine
- Peanut butter
- Jam
- Peanut butter and jam
- Other spreads

Mid-Tier: Breakfast Burrito

A Canadian classic, good at all times of the day.

- Scrambled eggs
- Lettuce
- Shredded cheddar cheese
- Salsa

TOAST VARIATIONS (V)

Also called toasties.

If you live alone, you may struggle to finish a loaf of bread before it goes bad. This is where toast has a key benefit over ordinary bread. If you buy pre-sliced bread, you can store the bread in the freezer, take out one slice at a time, and defrost it in the toaster. This isn't a particularly Sad-Bastard life hack, because it's indistinguishable from toast made from non-frozen bread. This is the kind of life hack even well-adjusted folk need to know.

We suppose you could also make sandwiches, if you've got non-moldy bread on the counter or in the fridge instead of in the freezer. But that sounds unlikely.

Core Ingredients
* Bread
* Things that go on toast

Preparation
* Apply bread to toaster.
* When toast pops, remove from toaster.
* Put stuff of choice on toast.
* Optional: put another slice of toast on top to make a "closed-face" sandwich instead of an "open-faced" sandwich.

Variations
There are nearly infinite toast variations.

* Butter or margarine
* Peanut butter
* Nutella
* Marshmallow fluff

- Maple syrup "butter"
- Banana slices with any of the above
- Butter or margarine & chocolate sprinkles are popular in the Netherlands.
- Jam
- Peanut butter & jam
- Cheese
- *The Humble Egg* in any cooked form
- Cheese & jam
- Cheese & egg
- Hummus
- Baked beans from a can, warmed in the microwave. *Beans on toast are popular in the UK.*
- Avocado slices

Pro-tip: If you're feeling really good, make part-baked bread rolls you bought from the frozen section, but that's pretty damn ambitious.

CRACKERS AND STUFF

Core Ingredients
* Crackers, any type.

Preferably Night Beats.

Preparation
* Eat the crackers out of the box while watching bad reruns on TV.

Variations
* Anything that's good on toast is good on crackers.
* You shouldn't put the crackers in the toaster.

FANCY CHEESE AND CRACKERS

This will impress a guest, possibly because it involves actual cooking.

Core Ingredients
* Brie or Camembert cheese. The cheapest you can find is perfect.
* Crackers, any type.

Preparation I: By the Wheel
* You're gonna fully melt the cheese, so you need it to have a rind to contain it in the oven.
* Ideally your baking dish has edges so it acts as an extra layer of containment. Especially if you pour a liquid like maple syrup on top before baking.
* Put in the oven at 350°F or 175°C. It'll probably take about 15 minutes.
* Serve with crackers. Guests will expect a knife to spread the cheese on the crackers but you can dip if you're not a coward.

Preparation II: By the Cracker
* Put slices of the cheese on crackers on a baking tray.
* Put in the oven at 350°F or 175°C for just long enough to make the cheese melty. Maybe 5 minutes?

Variations
Add any of these on top of the cracker or the cheese before baking.

* Maple syrup.
* Dried cranberries.
* Walnuts or other nuts.
* Jam. *Peach jam and chopped habanero peppers are a particularly good flavour combination with brie, and you can feel fancy eating it!*

HUMMUS (V)

Hummus is awesome because it tastes good, it's highly portable, and it's even healthy and full of protein. *You can buy it discounted from the store on your way to the activist potluck. Unless Ian from Cascade bought the last marked-down tub.*

Core Ingredients
* Hummus from the store.
* Carrots. Baby carrots or adult carrots: the choice is yours.

Preparation
Some people say you need to peel adult carrots. They are liars. Washing them is good—dirt has a terrible texture.

* Dip carrots into hummus.
* Eat.

Variations
* If you are feeling more ambitious, there are other vegetables to dip into the hummus. Peppers. Celery, if you must.
* Add a dash of olive oil and a spice like thyme or chili to the top of your hummus to be a Fancy Sad Bastard.
* Dip cheese into hummus.
* Dip tortilla chips or pita chips.
* Spread hummus on bread or toast.
* Use hummus as a sauce over pasta or rice.
* Hummus is also great eaten off a spoon standing in front of the fridge.

GARLIC BREAD Ⓥ

Garlic bread will improve your mood. It's scientifically proven. By which we mean, Blythe from The Sleep of Reason trilogy likes it, and she's a scientist.

Core Ingredients
* Bread
* Garlic (powdered is fine)
* Some type of oil-substance. Butter, margarine, vegetable oil, olive oil. All good.

Preparation
* Take bread.
* Put oil-substance (butter, margarine, vegetable oil, or olive oil) on the non-crust part of the bread.
* Put garlic on top. This could be powdered garlic, garlic squeezed from a tube, maybe even freshly minced garlic. If you're using something liquid (melted butter/margarine or oil), you can mix the garlic in with it for easier spreading.
* Ideally, bake in the oven at 350°F (175°C) until hot and deliciously toasty. We recommend wrapping it up in tinfoil first, but this is not compulsory.
* If using the oven is too much for today, you can microwave it instead to melt the margarine and heat the bread. No one can stop you.

Become ungovernable.

Variations
* You can make this on really fancy bread like on a baguette or on part-baked rolls from the freezer. Or on slices of whatever loaf is in your freezer.
* Put cheese on top before you cook it.
* You don't actually need to heat the bread when making garlic bread. It's delicious at room temperature.
* If you're having a great day, make extra and freeze it before it's baked. You can wrap it in tin foil for the freezer like a fancy grocery store would. Then you've got garlic bread on hand to bake for emergencies.

Emergencies like hungry vampires?

TOSTADAS CON TOMATE (V)

This meal sounds much fancier if you don't know enough Spanish to translate it as tomatoes on toast.

Core Ingredients
* Bread
* Tomatoes
* Salt
* Olive oil or butter or margarine or mayonnaise

Preparation I: Sliced Tomatoes
* Toast bread.
* Spread butter, margarine, or mayonnaise on the toast—or drizzle olive oil over it.
* Add tomato slices.
* Sprinkle with salt.
* Optional: add a second slice of toast on top.

Preparation II: Grated Tomatoes
* Toast bread.
* Drizzle toast with olive oil.
* Grate the tomato with the cheese grater so you get a tomato mush. You want to do this over a plate, not over the kitchen counter.
* Put the tomato mush on the bread.
* Sprinkle with salt.
* If you've got dried oregano, sprinkle that on too.

GRILLED CHEESE SANDWICHES

Core Ingredients
* Bread
* Cheese
* Butter or margarine or oil if you're making this in a frying pan

If you use American cheese singles, you don't need to slice the cheese yourself. But on the downside, then you need to eat American cheese singles.

Preparation: Do This No Matter What
* Put sliced cheese between two sides of bread.

Preparation I: Microwave
* Put on a plate and microwave until the cheese is melty.

Preparation II: Oven
* Spread butter or margarine on both sides of the bread.
* Put on a baking tray and bake in the oven at 400°F or 200°C until the cheese is melty. This should take only 5 minutes or so.
* Flip the sandwich halfway through cooking.

Preparation III: Frying Pan
* Put a wee bit of oil or margarine or butter in the pan and put the stove on low or medium heat.
* Cook the sandwich until one side of the bread is crispy, then flip it and cook the other side. You can add more margarine when you flip it so both sides get some. Try to pay some attention so that you flip it before the bread turns to charcoal.
* If you put a lid or large plate on the pan, the cheese will get extra melty.

Preparation IV: Grilled-Cheese Machine
Grilled-cheese machines exist (for under $20). They don't foolproof it, but

they make sealed grilled cheese as long as a) you line up the cheese and bread perfectly and b) you unplug them when the light goes off. If either of these points are not observed, cheese bubbles out and you have to clean the grilled-cheese maker. Or you could just throw it out and buy another one, they're so cheap and the frustration is so great from some cheese messes.

* Put a slice of white squishy soft crusted bread on bottom of machine in appropriate slots.
* Put slices of cheese precisely on top of bread so none falls over the edges of the bread. *If any does, tear it off like a wild animal and eat it as a prize, or add it on top of the cheese slice for an extra cheese pocket.*
* Line up the other slice of fluffy, squishy, soft crusted bread on top of the cheese.
* Close the machine and plug in.
* When the light goes green and you hear the ding, unplug immediately and *carefully* remove your sandwiches

Variations
* Slice diagonally.
* Slice vertically.
* Slice horizontally you absolute Lord of Chaos.
* Pair with ketchup.
* Add fried onions inside the sandwich.
* Add jam inside the sandwich.
* Add avocado inside the sandwich.
* Add thinly sliced apple inside the sandwich.
* Add spices like everything-bagel seasoning or dried garlic to the sandwich.
* If you're making it in a frying pan, spread a little bit of mayo on both outsides of the sandwich. Sounds gross, but it's incredible.
* Pairing with tomato soup is a classic!
* Don't include the top slice of bread—make an open-faced melted cheese sandwich instead. Not recommended in a grilled-cheese machine.

"PIZZA" Ⓥ

This is much, much tastier if you make it in the oven than the microwave. But it's still good in the microwave, and the nutritional content is the same.

Core Ingredients

- Bread-like substance. Bagels are highly encouraged, but pita bread is great here too. *We've heard that it's even possible to make this using pizza dough, but that sounds fake.*

  You can use any wheat and wheat by-products if the Sheriff's Secret Police don't catch you.

- Tomato sauce
- Cheese

  Vegan cheese would work here, but the tastiest vegan cheeses are often kinda expensive. Or you could omit the cheese entirely.

Preparation

- Take a bagel or other bread-like-substance.
- Put tomato-based pasta sauce on top.
- Put cheese on top, if you're using cheese.
- Cook in the microwave in 30-second intervals or in the oven until the cheese melts and/or the bagel is hot. *If you're cooking this in the oven, put the pizza bagel in the oven on broil, but don't go anywhere! Broil will melt the cheese and cook the bagel to a delicious crispiness very fast, so keep a close eye on it. For our Irish friends, broil is Very Hot. Use 200°C.*

Variations

- Italian spice mix on top of the pasta sauce is the secret ingredient of top-quality pizza bagels.
- Anything you like to eat on pizza can go on a pizza bagel.

Clarke from The Things We Couldn't Save, I'm sharing the information with the world. The people need to know.

112

TANZANIAN BRAISED COCONUT CABBAGE (V)

This is the kind of real recipe which has real measurements. Feel free to ignore them. We do.

Core Ingredients

* One red onion. The colour is nice but not essential.
* Cooking oil (¼ cup or a few glugs from the bottle)
* Cabbage (whole cabbage, ideally pre-cut into 1-inch wedges)
* Coconut milk (1 cup but realistically just put in the whole can)
* Salt
* Pepper

Preparation

* Chop a red onion, unless you bought pre-chopped onion.
* Chop a cabbage into pieces, unless you were able to buy a pre-chopped cabbage.
* In a large saucepan, sauté onions in all the oil until soft.
* Add cabbage and cook, stirring, until cabbage loses its crispness.
* Stir in coconut milk and season with salt and pepper.
* Simmer for 5 minutes.

Variations

* You can make this with most other vegetables, fresh or frozen.
* Serve with _Rice_ or _Couscous._

BAG SALAD Ⓥ

This is easy to make, but it assumes you have lettuce in the fridge. Salad greens go bad fast. You probably went to the grocery store recently to cook this.

Is salad really cooking? What is the nature of time and reality?

Core Ingredients and Supplies
- Pre-chopped lettuce or other salad greens. These usually come in a bag.
- Salad dressing. Some bags of salad come with a salad dressing inside. That's one less decision you have to make.

Preparation I
- Put salad greens onto the plate or into the bowl you plan to eat from.
- Add toppings as desired.
- Pour on salad dressing.

Preparation II: Elite Salad Hack
- Shove lettuce and toppings into a Ziploc bag.
- Add dressing.
- Close bag.
- Shake.
- Consume. The contents, not the bag.

Variations
- Add nuts.
- Add seeds.
- Add dried fruit.
- Add fresh fruit.
- Add canned beans. Probably chickpeas.
- Add olives.

- ★ Add cheese. Feta, blue cheese, or cheddar are tops in salad.
- ★ Add black beans, guacamole, and salsa to make a taco salad.
- ★ If you're feeling fancy, chop up whatever fresh vegetables are in the fridge.

God-Tier
- ★ Pour olive oil over the salad, then pour any vinegar over the salad. Voilà! Homemade salad dressing. *Pre-mixing the salad dressing by shaking the components together in a jar is nice, but unnecessary. And you'd need to wash the jar.*
- ★ This also works with lemon juice instead of vinegar.

Pro-tip: If you use olive oil & balsamic vinegar or lemon juice and then add sea salt, your guest will be incredibly impressed with your chef-ly prowess.

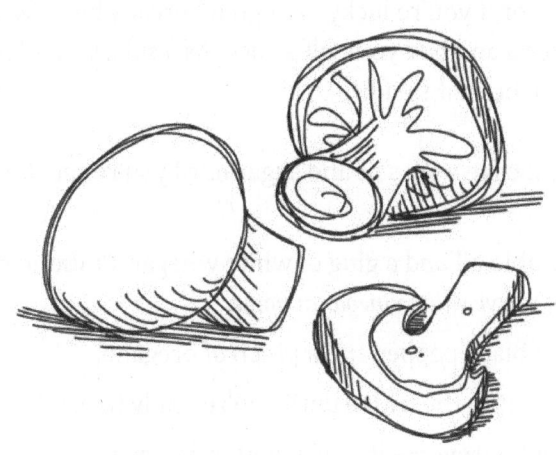

CABBAGE SALADS (V)

Cabbage salad three ways.

Core Ingredients
* Cabbage. You can grate it by hand or with a food processor, or just chop it with a knife into smallish pieces. Or buy it pre-shredded for a low-effort option.

Preparation I: Coleslaw
* Combine shredded cabbage with mayonnaise and a good glug of cider vinegar or rice vinegar. *Or use another type of vinegar. Whatever is in the house will work.*
* Optional: also grate in some carrots.
* Stir.
* Put it in the fridge until you're ready to eat it. It's tastier if you let it sit for at least half an hour.

Preparation II: Swedish Pizza Salad
If you travel to Sweden, or if you're lucky enough to already be in Sweden, you might go to a pizzeria and buy yourself a slice. As a side, you might order a "pizza salad." This will be that salad.

* Season shredded cabbage with salt and sugar until you're satisfied with the flavour.
* Add a glug of vegetable oil and a glug of white vinegar. *Or use another type of vinegar if you don't have white vinegar at home.*
* Add a good grind of black pepper and a pinch of oregano.
* Stir through and put it in the fridge until you're ready to eat it.
* This makes excellent leftovers—it's even better day two.

Preparation III: Bottom-Tier Japanese Addictive Cabbage

* Season shredded cabbage with the powder from your instant ramen noodles.
* Add a glug of rice vinegar or any other vinegar you've got around the house.
* Crumble raw ramen noodles into salad.
* Stir and consume.

Preparation IV: God-Tier Japanese Addictive Cabbage

Depending on where you live, you might be looking at a trip to an Asian grocery store to buy wonton-soup powder and Chinese sesame paste. If you can't get all these ingredients, you can mix-and-match from Bottom-Tier and God-Tier to make your own delicious salad variation.

* Season shredded cabbage with wonton-soup powder.
* Add Chinese sesame paste and rice vinegar.
* Add minced garlic or dried garlic flakes.
* Add sesame seeds. You can toast these first by heating them in a wee frying pan.
* Stir and enjoy.

ANTS ON A LOG (V)

Warning: this recipe includes raw celery. Only weirdos like raw celery.

Core Ingredients
* Celery sticks
* Peanut butter
* Raisins

Preparation
* Wash a celery stalk. Optionally cut it into two or three shorter celery sticks.
* Fill the curvy part in the middle with peanut butter. This is your "log."
* Put raisins on top of the peanut butter. These are your "ants."
* Eat.

FRIED PLANTAINS (V)

Plantains are great. Plus, when they go black, they're ready to eat. They're much more forgiving than bananas, which are kinda gross if you forget about them and they go black.

Core Ingredients
- Plantains
- Butter or margarine or cooking oil

Preparation
- Peel and slice the plantain.
- Add the butter to a frying pan.
- Fry over low or medium heat, flipping once so both sides get brown.
- Eat.

Plantains look similar to bananas, so we tried this with a banana, and it also tasted good. If only everything that looked similar tasted the same.

SMOOTHIE VARIATIONS ⓥ

Smoothies are excellent for those depressive episodes where you're too exhausted to function, as you can get calories and nutrients into your body without even bothering to chew.

Core Ingredients and Supplies

- Blender
- Fruit, like raspberries, blackberries, or strawberries. *We particularly recommend frozen fruit, as it's cheaper and lasts longer, and will make the smoothie cold and refreshing.*
- Juice or milk or some other liquid

Preparation

- Put fruit in the blender.
- Add some liquid.
- Blend.
- If it's too thick to blend, or if you want it less thick when you drink it, add more liquid.
- If it's not sweet enough, add sugar or honey or banana or something else that's sweet.

Variations

You can put almost anything in a smoothie. Will it blend? If you have a good blender, yes. Will it taste good? We leave this question as an exercise for the Reader.

- Banana, fresh
- Banana which you put in the freezer when you realised it was going black. You need to peel it, but you don't need to defrost it before you blend it.
- Frozen fruit

- ✱ Fresh fruit
- ✱ Yogurt
- ✱ Fresh or frozen avocado??
- ✱ Fresh or frozen spinach???
- ✱ Protein powder
- ✱ Chocolate powder
- ✱ Peanut butter
- ✱ Sugar
- ✱ Honey
- ✱ Maple syrup
- ✱ Other?????

Pro-tip: Washing blenders is really annoying unless you rinse them off right away when you're done using them. If you don't have the energy for this, consider letting them soak in water before you wash them. You can invest in something like a NutriBullet that is simpler to clean. If you really, really hate washing blenders, make something else.

ICE CREAM

Like smoothies, except you don't have to make it yourself or clean a blender.

Core Ingredients
* Ice cream. That's it.
* Get the vegan version if you don't eat dairy.

Preparation
* You can eat ice cream out of the tub.
* You don't even need a spoon.
* Those plastic knives will work in a pinch.
* If you peel the cardboard from around the top, you can eat it like a giant ice cream cone.

MOROCCAN ORANGES (V)

Actual Moroccan oranges with cinnamon are a delicious fancy dessert that also involves powdered sugar and orange blossom water. But you are a Sad Bastard and you can get that awesome taste with even lower effort. This genuinely tastes good and is an excellent source of Vitamin C.

Not today, scurvy. Not today.

Core Ingredients
- Oranges
- Cinnamon

Preparation
- Slice the oranges over a bowl so that none of the juice escapes. Ideally slice thinly. Don't bother peeling them yet.
- Sprinkle cinnamon in the bowl and stir the whole thing up.
- Let it sit for a bit. The juice and cinnamon will mix together to form a delicious goo-like substance which sticks to the orange slices.
- Take out the orange slices and sprinkle more cinnamon over them.
- Eat! You probably don't want to eat the peel.

Unless that's your thing, and who are we to stop you?

"BAKED" APPLES ⓥ

Technically, you could make this in the oven. If you wanted to.

Core Ingredients
* Apples
* Sugar
* Cinnamon

Preparation
* Cut apples into quarters and remove the cores.
* Put apple quarters in a bowl with a little bit of water in the bottom.
* Sprinkle sugar and cinnamon on top.
* Microwave 1 minute at a time until the apples are mushy.

Variations
* Goes well with ice cream.
* Goes well with yogurt.

BANANA FROZEN YOGURT

You know that thing where you freeze chunks of banana and then put them in a blender and make fake ice cream? This is that, but without the blender.

Core Ingredients
- Greek yogurt
- Bananas

Preparation
- Take a cup or so of Greek yogurt.
- Take two bananas or so.
- Mash them together with a fork, or a masher, or a blender if you've got one of those.
- Stick in the freezer.
- Stir with a fork after 40 minutes or so.
- Stir again every 40 mins or so until frozen solid and smooth. It's okay if you forget sometimes. This process probably takes three to five stirring sessions, so this is a "start it in the afternoon and it's ready by the evening" food.
- That's it. That's all you need to do.

Bottom-Tier
- Don't stir it. It's not actually necessary.

Variations
- Add some chocolate powder or chocolate sauce.

"PARFAIT"

Regardless of what ogres and donkeys say, not all parfaits have layers.

Core Ingredients
* Yogurt
* Store-bought cookies (or biscuits if you're Irish)
* Jam

Preparation
* Add yogurt and jam to your bowl.
* Crumble up cookies on top.
* Eat with a spoon.

Variations
* Defrost frozen fruit in the microwave and use that instead of jam.
* Or use fresh fruit.

Our professional-chef friend informed us this is closer to an Eton Mess than to a parfait, but really, isn't everything that comes out of Eton a disastrous mess?

CHOCOLATE PUDDING (V)

This recipe is good enough to serve to guests. It's good enough to include even though it has actual measurements. And we don't measure ingredients lightly. Or at all—we include a cheat underneath.

Core Ingredients
- ½ cup sugar
- ½ cup cocoa powder
- 3 Tbsp. cornstarch
- 2 cups water

Here's the thing. You can do this as ratios. For every 1 measure of cornstarch, add 3 of sugar, 3 of cocoa and 12 of water. This works no matter whether you use a tablespoon, or a cup, or a leftover cream-cheese tub as your measure. However, if you use a cup measure for your ratios, you'll need a very large bowl to hold the 19 cups of stuff.

Preparation
- Stir together the dry ingredients (everything besides the water).
- Add the water.
- More stir.
- Microwave for 1 minute then stir.
- Repeat until it's pudding.
- Put it in the fridge.
- Ideally wait until it gets to fridge temperature to eat it, but we don't judge. But it will taste even better. Promise.

Bottom-Tier

* You can use instant hot chocolate powder instead of a mix of sugar and cocoa. It might only work with specific brands of instant powder; we haven't tested it with every brand ever invented. In fact, we tested it only with the absolute cheapest store-brand instant hot chocolate powder, but the important thing is that it worked.

God-Tier

* Substitute milk or milk equivalent instead of water.
* Defrost frozen fruit. Add it to the pudding when it's done.
* Add fresh fruit to the pudding when it's done.

A note for our British friends: In Canada, pudding is a slightly thicker version of custard. We know that it means "any dessert" in your country. Your country has a lot to answer for already.

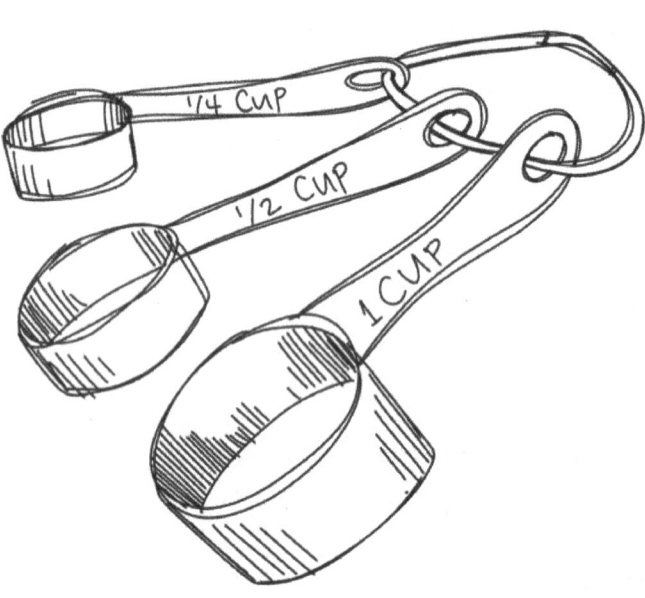

CORE INGREDIENTS TO KEEP IN YOUR KITCHEN

These are our top picks for what ingredients we keep in our kitchens at all times so we don't starve. Your list is probably different! But we thought you might be inspired by seeing our faves.

* **Frozen vegetables.** Frozen veg are vastly underrated. They've got the same nutritional content as fresh, they're pre-chopped, and they don't go bad in the fridge when you neglect them for weeks. You do pay more for quality. But there's nothing wrong with store-brand mixes, and they're cheaper than fresh too. We recommend keeping in the freezer three different kinds—**spinach**, **corn**, and a **vegetable mix**. But play around with different types. This is a choice with no bad options.

* **Ramen.** Or, if you're Irish, **instant noodles**.

* **Spices.** Spices exist for a reason, and that's to make sad food taste better and bad food last longer. We highly recommend **curry powder**, which is lots of spices mixed together to save you time. **Italian seasoning** is also a great mix. And **seasoning salt**—then you don't even need to add salt. **Pepper** is a classic. *Despite what the label says, most spices don't go off. If you can separate them and they smell good, they are probably fine to use.*

* **Garlic.** We are listing this separately from other spices because it's the best one. It comes in many different forms, from powdered (lasts forever), to tube (easy and mess free), to bottled minced, to frozen (also lasts forever), to fresh (most flavourful but you have to chop or press it). You can buy peeled garlic and save yourself some time. It also keeps vampires away, though only the bloodsucking kind and not the emotional kind.

  If you are a werewolf with a vampire girlfriend like Jane and Lilith from Night Beats, omit garlic.

* **Onions.** You can also get pre-chopped onions either fresh or frozen. It's more money, but less cutting and less crying.

  Counterpoint, cutting onions is a great way to cry without anyone judging you.

THE SAD BASTARD COOKBOOK

- **Salt.** Salt exists to make food less bland. Salt is a gift you give yourself.
- **Soy sauce.** Salt with flavour.
- **Couscous.** Or **instant rice.** Or **instant oatmeal.** Maybe all of these. You need a carb you can cook with nothing more complicated than a kettle, a bowl, and a spoon. *Bowl and spoon optional. Any watertight container and stirring implement will do. Empty yogurt tub and plastic knife, your moment has arrived.*
- **Some sort of cooking oil or spray.** We recommend the cheapest kind you can find. A basic olive oil makes a nice sauce, but if you're only buying one type of oil, canola oil is often cheapest and it fries things very well. As does a nice generic "vegetable oil." Butter or margarine also work here.
- **Nut, seeds, & dried fruit.** Nuts and seeds are tiny stores of healthy oils and protein. Plus they taste great. And they can go in basically anything, or you can eat them on their own, on your couch, as you read *Cascade*. A **nut mix** will have lots of them together, or buy your favourites separately. **Peanut, sunflower seeds,** and **raisins** are usually the cheapest.
- **Pasta sauce.** Whatever kind you like best. **Salsa** makes a remarkably good pasta sauce. Lots of types of **canned soup** also make good pasta sauces. Bonus, canned soup is also great for making soup!
- **Pasta.** Whatever shape you like best.
- **Cheddar cheese.** Yes it goes bad, eventually. No, it's not vegan. We're bad at following rules, even ones we make ourselves.
- **Bread and bread-like substances.** Did you know you can freeze bread? The texture can be wrong afterwards but, if so, you can fix it by toasting it. Defrost it by toasting it twice. Or defrost it on the counter and toast it once. We recommend **bread**, and/or **bagels.** *Get your wheat and wheat by-products.*
- **Something to spread on bread.** And to use with other things! Consider: **margarine, butter, mayonnaise, sandwich spread, jam, hummus.** Or others! The world is yours. At least the spreads aisle is yours.
- **Peanut butter.** The spread is so useful we listed it separately. We personally prefer the "peanuts only, crunchy" type. But unless you have a nut allergy, there are no bad options among the nut butters.

* **Canned beans.** Dried beans are cheaper than canned, but they take a lot more prep. Like, hours more. Canned beans are already plenty cheap. A **bean medley** will let you make bean salad, **lentils** make great soup, and **chickpeas** will enhance basically any dish. And other types are great too. *If you're prone to gas, the bean liquid can make you bloated, which feels like bad period cramps. Pour the liquid away and rinse the beans in the can. Rinsing them in a colander is more effective, but it makes another dish dirty. Conversely, if this isn't a problem for you, you can keep the liquid for aquafaba, which is a great vegan egg substitute.*

ZILLA'S SHOPPING LIST & WEEKLY MENU

Shopping list
- Peanut butter
- Jam
- Instant oatmeal
- Cereal
- Nut & raisin mix
- Cocoa powder
- Corn starch
- Sugar
- Cinnamon powder
- Curry powder
- Bread (store in the freezer)
- Tortilla wraps
- Plant milk
- Frozen mixed vegetables
- Frozen vegetarian spring rolls
- Rice
- Couscous
- Udon noodles
- Ramen
- Oil
- Soy sauce
- Sesame oil
- Salsa
- Canned minestrone soup (two cans)

- ✺ Canned lentils
- ✺ Canned black beans
- ✺ Sweet potato
- ✺ Plantains

Weekly Menu

Monday
Breakfast: Toast with peanut butter and jam.
Lunch: Ramen with no sides made using the work kettle.
Dinner: Lentils in a pot with curry powder, served over couscous. Make enough for leftovers.

Tuesday
Breakfast: Cereal with plant milk.
Lunch: Turn the leftover lentils and couscous into a wrap by wrapping it in the tortilla wrap.
Dinner: Rice and black beans with salsa. Make enough for leftovers.

Wednesday
Breakfast: Toast with peanut butter and jam.
Lunch: Turn the leftover rice and black beans with salsa into a wrap by wrapping it in the tortilla.
Dinner: Fried udon noodles with frozen vegetables, sesame oil, and soy sauce. Make enough for leftovers.

Thursday
Breakfast: Cereal with plant milk.
Lunch: Leftover fried noodles with frozen vegetables, sesame oil, and soy sauce.
Dinner: Couscous with nut & raisin mix and cinnamon powder. Make enough to have leftovers.

Friday
Breakfast: Toast with peanut butter and jam.
Lunch: Leftover couscous with nut & raisin mix and cinnamon powder.
Dinner: Rice mixed with canned soup and frozen vegetables. Make enough rice for leftovers.

Saturday
Breakfast: Instant oatmeal with cinnamon powder, peanut butter, and plant milk.
Lunch: Fried plantains.
Dinner: Leftover rice turned into fried rice with frozen mixed vegetables, soy sauce, and sesame oil. Served with spring rolls on the side. Chocolate pudding for dessert.

Sunday
Breakfast: Instant oatmeal with jam and nut & raisin mix.
Lunch: Canned soup.
Dinner: Sweet potato quesadillas (what we call a pumpki-dilla in this cookbook) served with salsa. Leftover chocolate pudding for dessert.

RACHEL'S "THREE MEALS A DAY ARE COGNITIVE OVERLOAD" SHOPPING LIST & WEEKLY MENU

Meal planning is a lot of work, and most of the time I can't manage to eat three meals a day. I sometimes buy a big box of energy bars and eat them for breakfast, but most of the time my breakfast is coffee. Is that healthy? Ehhh. I've lived to middle age like this.

My life is additionally complicated by a peanut butter ban in my workplace, so I generally substitute cashew or almond butter for the peanut butter.

Shopping list
- Cooking oil
- Soy sauce
- Sesame oil
- Hummus
- Tofu
- Coconut milk
- Ramen/Instant Noodles
- Instant rice
- Rice noodles
- Onions
- Garlic
- Chilies (any kind, though I'm partial to Thai bird's eye chilis)
- Curry powder or berbere
- Chickpeas
- Lentils
- Nut butter
- Pasta noodles

- ✺ Pasta sauce
- ✺ Tortilla wraps
- ✺ Chocolate chips
- ✺ Sugar or maple syrup
- ✺ Vegetables (pre-diced cabbage and whatever else you want, either fresh or frozen)
- ✺ Potato
- ✺ Bagged salad
- ✺ Salad dressing
- ✺ Various condiments of your choice, but maybe you already have these

Weekly Menu

Monday
Lunch: Hummus with crackers or carrots
Dinner: Ramen with various vegetables, soy sauce, and sesame oil
Dessert: Peanut butter balls with chickpeas, which you can eat as a snack or breakfast throughout the rest of the week

Tuesday
Lunch: Bagged salad with dressing
Dinner: Pasta with tomato sauce

Wednesday
Lunch: Leftover pasta
Dinner: Apocalypse ramen

Thursday
Lunch: Hummus wrap
Dinner: Lentils in a pot with berbere or curry powder. You can use chickpeas instead if you don't want to buy two types of beans. Make enough for tomorrow.

Friday
Lunch: Leftover lentils in a pot
Dinner: Rice with fresh or frozen vegetables (chop a bit of extra vegetables)

Saturday

Hey, you got up in time for breakfast! Go you!: Peanut butter balls with chickpeas

Lunch: Tanzanian braised cabbage served over instant rice (save some of the cabbage!)

Dinner: Baked potato with garlic and oil (make 2 and save one for tomorrow morning)

Sunday

Brunch: Bubble and squeak

Dinner: Cheater chana masala served over instant rice (make enough for some lunches next week)

THANK YOU TO OUR CONTRIBUTORS

It takes a village to write a cookbook. We want to thank the following people who suggested recipes, beta read and tested meals, and supported us during the book-making process.

Special thank you to Rohan O'Duill, who assisted us as both an author and a professional chef, despite his abject horror at most of the recipes in this book. This isn't the kind of food he cooks in his kitchen, but he still managed to make the recipes both simpler and tastier. We couldn't have written this book without him.

To Nicole Northwood, fixer of words, contributor of recipes, marketing expert, and mentor in the intimidating world of publishing. The fact that this book is in your hands shows what a kick-ass teacher she is.

To our editors. Victoria Rose (Flickering Words) and Lindsay Hobbs (Topaz Literary) saw our project and asked us if we needed editors—simply because they believed in what we were trying to create. The best part of working with Victoria was having an editor with high-level cooking expertise. She knew what we were trying to express, so she was able to edit for clarity of cooking instructions, as well as for language errors. Lindsay formatted all our headings, subheadings, and footnotes so they had consistent styles, turning our ramblings into a structured book. Both were able to see our errors when repetition meant the words on the page no longer possessed meaning to our very tired eyes. We are so immensely grateful, both for the invaluable edits but also the vote of confidence in our work from the offer itself.

To Rysz Merey, excellent friend and supremely dedicated formatter. We thought turning this cookbook into an epub was the Kobayashi Maru scenario of layout, but you managed to cut through the Gordian Knot, to mix our metaphors like we'd mix a pot of soup.

To our tireless team of proofreaders: Anna Borisovskaya, Emma Berglund, Nicole Northwood, and Rysz Merey. Your eyes were so helpful, especially after we pulled all nighters and couldn't read our own words anymore.

To the many people who contributed recipes, and to our tireless beta testing team, who turned this from a series of jokes into workable instructions. Anna Borisovskaya, china shop, CJ Mantel, Clare, Emma Berglund, Eric Hortop, Fallopia Tuba, Franklin P. Smearcase, Gretchen McSomething, Holly, IJ Barry, Kayt Kismet, Lcohen, Lindsay Hobbs, Naomi, Naraht, Nye, omniamutantur, Rachel Corsini, Raye Frenzy, Renee Carignan, Sabitha Furiosa, Shannon Massey, S. M. Berry, Sun Salute, Tetsab, Tim & Rachel, Val, and Vicki Rosenzweig. And to the anonymous contributors, who are just as wonderful as the rest but much more mysterious.

To Reccia Mandelcorn, for agreeing to a last-minute pickle photoshoot.

To our Discord servers, who are endlessly loved and loving. *Night Beets, The Spicy Pepper (the Joy/Sad Unit), Cats and Eldritch Horrors,* and *LGBTQIA+ Critique Group.* And thank you to the many people who supported our vision along the way. If you marked the book as "to read" on Goodreads, offered us an encouraging word on a Discord server, e-mailed to say that you knew someone this book would help—that it might help you—we are so grateful.

And last but never least, to the many cats who contributed to this book, whether by screaming, walking over keyboards, or emotional support. All cats are beautiful, but you are the best.

MESSAGE FROM THE AUTHORS

The electronic version of this cookbook is free because, regardless of life circumstances, people deserve good food. If we and our community can help people with that, we want to. Even if it's as little as sharing recipe ideas.

That said, the *Night Beats* community contains a lot of authors. Including us! We authored the cookbook you're reading *right now*. And some other stuff too. Rachel A. Rosen published a climate fantasy novel [Cascade (The Sleep of Reason Book 1)](#) and Zilla Novikov has a satire novella, [Query](#). And [Marten's](#) got some great steampunk pilots. You might like them. You like books, right?

If you want to support us, here's some things you could do to help us as authors which don't cost money.

- You could share this book with a friend who could use it.
- You could share this book with your mortal enemy, kicking off a rom-com-style enemies-to-lovers montage.
- You could subscribe to our newsletter at https://nightbeatseu.ca/newsletter/
- You could write a review of this book. Books with more reviews on websites get recommended to more readers. [Goodreads](#), [Storygraph](#), [Amazon](#), Barnes & Noble, they're all good. Write a review telling our bot overlords that you like this book, and the algorithm will tell total strangers that they might like it too.
- God-Tier: Ask a librarian to buy our books for your local library. You

141

THE SAD BASTARD COOKBOOK

could use this as a free way to read and review our other books too! However, this may involve speaking to a librarian, and we cannot advocate approaching these malevolent beings in the flesh. Only if there is an online form.

But honestly, we don't need any of that.
Enjoy the cookbook. Know you're not alone. Share our coping mechanisms. Take care of yourself as much as you can.

NOT AN INDEX

So here's the deal: Indexes exist because back in the day, it was impossible to use a search function to look for recipes in a cookbook which used a specific ingredient. If you wanted to know how many of the recipes in this book involve peanut butter, you turned to the back of the book—this section right here—and you looked up the answer.

That was back in the day when books came on paper, and no one had cell phones, and you weren't allowed to use slide rules in math class. Hard times. But society has moved on. This is the future. Use the search function. If you only have the paper version of this book, you can get a free e-version on our website, www.nightbeatseu.ca.

If you need to look up how to parboil something, congratulations! You're probably feeling better enough that you don't need this cookbook. Use Google for that. Or Bing.

ABOUT THE CREATORS

Zilla Novikov screams into the void on a regular basis. When she's on Tumblr as zillanovikov, the void screams back. When she's writing for the Night Beats blog and newsletter (www.nightbeatseu.ca), the void gives her a high five. You can find her satirical novella Query at www.traumbooks.com.

Rachel A. Rosen is an activist, graphic designer, and for her sins, a high school teacher. Through magic dark as Vantablack, she has somehow conjured the time to write a book series, *The Sleep of Reason*. Check out her first novel, *Cascade,* at bppress.ca or, you know, the other online places books are sold. Find her on Instagram @rachelarosen, or visit her website rachelrosen.ca.

Marten Norr is a queer sci-fi/fantasy writer, full-time artist, purveyor of weird stuff, and little herald of chaos. He's famous on TikTok for 1) single-handedly destroying his grandmother's legacy, and 2) making the world aware that the reason there are so few mummies left in the world is because the Victorians ate them all. Learn more tru fax from Marten on Twitter at and Tiktok @flowerprinceart and check out his writing on Twitter @MartenNorr.

www.ingramcontent.com/pod-product-compliance
Ingram Content Group UK Ltd.
Pitfield, Milton Keynes, MK11 3LW, UK
UKHW021048070725
6753UKWH00057B/1651